BEYOND THE LAW

Books by James A. Pike

BEYOND THE LAW

A NEW LOOK IN PREACHING

OUR CHRISTMAS CHALLENGE

THE NEXT DAY

DOING THE TRUTH—A SUMMARY OF CHRISTIAN ETHICS

IF YOU MARRY OUTSIDE YOUR FAITH

BEYOND ANXIETY

CASES AND OTHER MATERIALS ON
NEW FEDERAL AND CODE PROCEDURE

Co-Author of

MAN IN THE MIDDLE

THE CHURCH, POLITICS AND SOCIETY

ROADBLOCKS TO FAITH

THE FAITH OF THE CHURCH

ADMINISTRATIVE LAW

Editor of

MODERN CANTERBURY PILGRIMS

BEYOND THE LAW

The Religious and Ethical Meaning of the Lawyer's Vocation

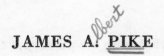

JAMES A. PIKE

The Rosenthal Lectures for 1962
Northwestern University Law School

Doubleday & Company, Inc.
Garden City, New York, 1963

Grateful acknowledgment for permission to quote is made to:

CANON GEORGE E. DeMILLE for an excerpt from *Man at Work in God's World*.

INDIANA UNIVERSITY PRESS for an excerpt from *The Moral Decision* by Edmond Cahn.

DAVID McKAY COMPANY, INC., for excerpts by Richard S. M. Emrich and Whitney North Seymour from *Man at Work in God's World*, edited by George E. DeMille. Copyright © 1956 by The Diocese of Albany. Courtesy of David McKay Company, Inc.

UNIVERSITY OF COLORADO for an excerpt from the Report of the Boulder Conference on Education of Lawyers for Their Public Responsibilities. Used by permission of Edward C. King, Dean, University of Colorado.

Scripture used throughout is from the Revised Standard Version, except for the Psalms, which are from the Book of Common Prayer.

To
ROBERT M. KINGSLEY
and
CHARLES E. CLARK

*who for the author were
among the great law professors
who informed and inspired—
and helped develop the critical spirit*

Contents

Foreword

The opportunity that what follows might be fruitful is due to the establishment in 1919 of the Julius Rosenthal Foundation, administered by the Northwestern University Law School, in memory of an eminent and beloved member of the Chicago Bar. It would be false modesty for the author if he were not to record his appreciation that he has been included in the company of the distinguished lawyers and scholars who have presented stimulating ideas at the School and widened the value of their words by publication. The invitation to participate in this series has meant more to me perhaps than to the other invitees in that it gave me reassurance that I am not regarded as one who deserted the great profession to which I gave my oath of allegiance a little more than a quarter of a century ago. Over the years, friendly fellow lawyers have been kind enough to say either that I am still practicing, but in a higher jurisdiction, or that now I have a different Client. To the degree to which this latter analysis is true, I hope that I have in these lectures sufficiently served this Client so that He rather than the author becomes the focus for the reader.

Since in these pages it will become apparent that I am an existentialist, it is quite in character for me to assert that one does not lecture in the abstract: in my extemporaneous presentation I was much aided by a supportive and concerned audience. Hence my thanks to all who came. And my thanks to Professor Vance N. Kirby, the chairman of the committee on arrangements, under whose wife, Harriet, I served on the editorial staff of the *Southern California Law Review* years ago, and whose first-born was the first child I baptized after my ordination to the ministry. They were a great help throughout. And thanks, too, to the distinguished Dean of the School, Dr. John Ritchie, whose warmth and interest contributed much to my output. These and others made the experience a very fine time; I hope this shows up in the pages that follow. One final credit: thanks to Mrs. Ruth Dunavon and Miss Grace Holcomb, of my own staff, who assisted in the preparation of the manuscript for publication, and to Harold W. Petersen, sound consultant at our Cathedral, who very much clarified the tape recordings of the addresses.

I have had the privilege of speaking at various law schools and to various Bar Associations on the general subject of these lectures. But my real preparation for speaking in a more disciplined way in this lectureship came to me because of the invitation to join the Committee of the American Association of Law Schools for the preparation of *Selected Readings on the Legal Profession*.[1] My particular task was the preparation of a selection of materials on the same subject as these lectures. The very fact of this invitation expressed the growing yearning for a larger sense of meaning in the practice of our profession. As to this present work, most of the quotations come from materials I collected for the closing chapter of the *Selected Readings*. Particularly encouraging to me in the task was the chairman of the A.A.L.S. committee, Professor John S. Bradway, formerly of Duke University Law School and now, in his retirement, adorning the faculty of Hastings College of the Law, University of California.

In an undertaking of this kind, one appreciates the words of John Donne: "No man is an *Island,* intire of it selfe." We are all interlocked, no matter what our calling. And all men are under call. One could write the same sort of book about the practice of medicine, nuclear development, public relations or retreading tires. But I am a priest and an attorney; hence I have written it this way.

JAMES A. PIKE

The Cathedral Close, San Francisco
Feast of the Transfiguration, 1962

[1] St. Paul, Minnesota: West Publishing Company, 1962.

The Rosenthal Lectures

1927, Sir William Searle Holdsworth, Vinerian Professor of Law, Oxford University

1928, Antonio Sanchez de Bustamente, University of Havana, member of the Permanent Court of International Justice

1929, John C. H. Wu, formerly Chief Justice of the Court of Appeals at Shanghai, and member of the Law Codification Commission of China

1931, Jean Escarra, of the Faculty of Law of the University of Paris

1934, Charles Warren, author of *The Supreme Court in United States History*

1936, Walton Hale Hamilton, Professor of Law, Yale University

1937, Henry T. Lummus, Associate Justice, Supreme Judicial Court of Massachusetts

1940, Lon L. Fuller, Professor of Law, Harvard University

1946–48, A series of lectures directed by Adlai E. Stevenson, presently United States Ambassador to the United Nations

1948–49, John N. Hazard, Professor, Russian Institute, Columbia University; Paul A. Freund, Professor of Law, Harvard University

1950, John P. Dawson, Professor of Law, University of Michigan

1951, Abraham H. Feller, General Counsel, United Nations

1952, Charles Horsky, member of the District of Columbia Bar

1952–53, Eugene Pepin, Legal Director, International Civil Aeronautics Organization; Arthur T. Vanderbilt, Chief Justice of the Supreme Court of New Jersey; Robert H. Jackson, Associate Justice of the Supreme Court of the United States; Walter V. Schaefer, Justice of the Supreme Court of Illinois; Herbert Wechsler, Professor of Law, Columbia University

1954, Adolf A. Berle, Jr., Professor of Law, Columbia University

1955, James Willard Hurst, Professor of Law, University of Wisconsin

1955–56, Louis B. Sohn, Professor of Law, Harvard University; Ernest A. Gross, Legal Adviser to the Secretary General of the United Nations; John J. Parker, Chief Judge of the United States Court of Appeals for the Fourth Circuit

1956–57, Nobushige Ukai, Professor of Law and Political Science, Tokyo University; A. E. Papale, Dean, School of Law, Loyola University, New Orleans; Herbert L. A. Hart, Professor of Jurisprudence, Oxford University

1958, Leon Green, formerly Dean of the Northwestern University Law School and presently Distinguished Professor of Law, University of Texas

1959, Louis Eisenstein, member of the District of Columbia Bar

1960, The Right Honorable Lord Radcliffe, Lord of Appeal in Ordinary of the United Kingdom

1961, Professor Harold C. Havighurst, former Dean of the Law School and presently a member of the faculty

1962, The Rt. Rev. James A. Pike, Bishop of the Episcopal Diocese of California and member of the California Bar

I

Introduction

About a decade ago I first expressed myself on the general subject of this book before a joint meeting of the Sections on Legal Education and on Bar Examinations of the American Bar Association. To raise the fundamental question, I set forth a hypothetical case:

At the time it was a buyer's market as far as legal talent was concerned. A promising young lawyer in a leading firm (who had good prospects of becoming a partner) was presented with a difficult decision. He was asked to draw up the papers for a corporate reorganization, which, as was assured by his study and the opinion of his seniors, was perfectly "legal." It was clear, too, that his and the firm's involvement in the matter was entirely within the canons of legal ethics. Yet as he took in the entire situation, it became evident to him that the whole deal was essentially a gyp: the arrangement proposed would be harmful to legitimate interests and to persons.

Where lay his duty? It was not unreasonable to sup-

pose that should he simply refuse to proceed on general
moral grounds that he would lose his job, or at least em-
barrass his future chances with the firm. This was not to
be dismissed as simply a selfish concern. First, he had an
obligation to feed his family, and he had no private
means; and, second—while this seems to be a rationalization, it still had a real basis in truth—if by playing
along on such things now he could reach the status of a
partner he would then have a real voice in the policy of
the firm as to co-operation or non-co-operation in the ends
of clients such as the ones involved here. (It is true that
perhaps by the time he reached a senior partnership he
might have compromised to a point that he would no
longer be sensitive—as he was now—to such questions;
nevertheless, as in politics, young men can be sincere
about such considerations.) On the other hand, in this
particular matter, he would find himself collaborating in
evil—and not abstract evil only, but evil affecting particular persons right now. What to do?

In presenting the illustration, I was not prepared to offer the answer. I was merely intending to raise a basic
question. But no sooner had I stated the case than a
distinguished pillar of the Bar, himself a partner in a
leading firm, rose and said: "But there is no question." I
interrupted to say that I had no answer to propose, but
I thought there was a question. He reasserted there was
no question and said: "A young man is supposed to do
what he is paid for!" I answered, "I had not realized how
close our profession is to the world's oldest profession."
Now, if he was right, and there is no question, then the
1962 Rosenthal Lectures are over at this point. But I am
proceeding on the basis that there is a question. Yet, right

away I must warn you that there is no precise answer to this particular question or to any number of analogous questions.

First, there is no answer from statutes, the common law or the canons of legal ethics. What we are talking about are the problems of the lawyer's professional life once these things have all been checked out. Here we can gain illumination from the Parable of the Pharisee and the Publican. Today we tend to use the word Pharisee as a definition of an insincere or hypocritical person. Actually such an attribution is unfair to the Pharisees and it misses the point of Jesus' rather persistent quarrel with those of this sect. The Pharisees were really earnest in keeping the rules—dozens and dozens of them. To use the illustrations in the familiar Parable, the Pharisee tithed, that is, gave one tenth of all that he possessed. There is no reason to believe that he really didn't. As a matter of fact, it is a pretty good idea, as I have come especially to realize as an administrator in the organized Church. To continue the illustrations in the Parable, he claimed that he prayed twice daily, and he probably really did—a good idea for any of us. And he claimed that he fasted; certainly a disciplined program for life is wise for any of us. So far, no hypocrisy or unsoundness. The difficulty was the Pharisee felt that when he kept all the rules, he was through— he had exhausted his moral obligation.

Now the statutes, the common law and the canons of legal ethics supply rules, scores of rules, analogous to those kept by the Pharisee. We assume conformity to these. But as to the area we will be considering in these chapters, we will gain no help from the established regulations. We will simply assume that these are being kept and ask, "Then what?" In seeking to answer this question, we can expect from the statutes, the common law and the canons help only by analogy.

Second, we expect no help from decisions in particular cases. If the lawyer is within the law, even right up to the edge of it, there is nothing to litigate, either on trial or on appeal.

Can we expect help from religion and ethics? Yes and no. We will not, according to my view, receive any specific answers from any religiously based code of ethics or, for that matter, from any humanist-based one. No system of ethics can find a pigeonhole for every life situation. It is something else we hope to gain from that dimension. As I said some years ago in an article in the *Northwestern University Law Review*,[1] the difficulty with natural law —to which we might hope to look for specific help in such situations—is that if it is stated narrowly enough to bring something to bear on specific problems it is not universal enough to qualify as natural law, but as mere temporal tradition; and if it is stated generally enough to escape that difficulty, it is not precise enough to give us answers.

What we may seek from a religio-ethical or world view is more of an understanding of the nature of the problem itself and the motivations and norms that may inspire the individual, the conscientious individual, in the specific task of resolving the specific situations with which he is confronted. This is what I mean by the ethic "Beyond the Law."

[1] Reviewing John C. H. Wu's *Fountain of Justice. Northwestern University Law Review*, Volume 51, No. 6, January–February 1957, pages 807–812.

II

The Public Image of the Lawyer

First, it should be asked, why do we lawyers care about our public image? If a given lawyer is doing well, should he care too much about a general public image? There are at least two reasons why we should care.

First, just plain pride in our profession. This is signified in our various law school buildings and in the various elements of their decor—things that Dean Wigmore (one of my distinguished predecessors in this lectureship) and others have collected to adorn the walls of the halls. These keep reminding us that we do—or should—have pride in our profession.

But there is an additional reason. It is well stated in the Preamble to the *Canons of Professional Ethics of the New York State Bar Association:*

. . . the future of the Republic, to a great extent, depends upon our maintenance of Justice pure and unsullied. It cannot be so maintained unless the conduct and the motives of the members of our pro-

fession are such as to merit the approval of all just
men.

What is our public image?

A burlesque of it is presented by the story of the three
professionals shipwrecked on a raft within sight of a
South Pacific island. The raft showed no signs of floating
in to the island and all attempts at signaling the citizens
of the island seemed of no avail. Any one of them—
pressed by the threat of starvation—would gladly have
swum ashore, except for the fact that the waters were
shark-infested. Nevertheless, it was apparent to all three
that one must take the chance. Lots were cast, and
the adventurer chosen was an attorney. As he dived from
the raft with some trepidation and headed rapidly for
the shore, the other two noticed a marvelous thing. The
sharks that they saw in the clear blue water separated
to either side of him and the swimmer reached the beach
unscathed. When he returned with help, in the form of
a secure boat manned by two natives, they immediately
asked him how all this happened. "Simply professional
courtesy," he answered.

The reason such a story is told and the reason it is
funny is that there is something to it.

One other extreme, but suggestive, illustration is af-
forded by Alfred Rothschild:

Not long ago a friend and I were discussing some
aspects of the McClellan Committee hearings, and
in particular the effect of the TV broadcasts with
their procession of tight-lipped deadpan witnesses
and their attorneys. "When I see and hear these
birds," said my friend, "I can't help thinking of some-

thing from Shakespeare. Not that I am much of a hand at quoting from him, but this thing has always stuck in my memory. It's what Dick the Butcher said to Rebel Jack Kade: 'The first thing we do, let's kill all the lawyers!' "[1]

And he adds the comment that though he did not like to hear this from a layman, "it does seem clear that the 'birds' could not have developed their socially vicious schemes, their trick contracts, their entire corporate and other setups without a great deal of legal assistance. And it seems equally clear that their attorneys in accepting substantial fees for their services are, in effect, associated with the enterprises and deriving an income from their operation."

In a considerably earlier period, President Woodrow Wilson, hardly a gentleman given to extreme statements, said in an address to the American Bar Association in 1910: "Lawyers are not now regarded as mediators of progress. Society was always ready to be prejudiced against them; now it finds its prejudice confirmed."

These quotations are utilized not as a total or adequate evaluation of our profession, but simply to suggest that in the eyes of the public the image of our profession has become somewhat dimmed.

There was a day in the development of our country when the picture of the lawyer was of the utmost significance in the eyes of the public. There has been a change. What are the reasons for the change? There are at least five:

---

[1] From "Ethics and the Lawyer" (1958, unpublished). Mr. Rothschild is a member of the New York Bar.

1. A factor always operative and increasingly important is the fact that the attorney is generally drawn in
at points of controversy and of frustration, and thus, for
psychological reasons, often becomes a scapegoat for the
venting of feelings on the part of one or of both clients.
The legal profession is not unique in being the object of
such reactions. It happens to the pastor or the psychiatrist
or the social worker—to any professional who is brought
in when things are already in a mess, where the situation
is already tense, and where personal feelings or, even
when things seem coldly impersonal, where personal or
corporate purposes are threatened with blockage or frustration. This type of psychological reaction has continued
to mount in a society where the increasing complexity of
interrelationships and pressures increase the chances that
particular intentions may be inhibited in whole or in
part. All this works toward increasing controversy and
partisanship, and thus it is increasingly inevitable that
lawyers are not going to be universally liked.

2. Due to increasing specialization in practice (especially in large urban communities, but more and more
even in smaller places) the lawyer less and less has the
role of a general "wise man," a general counselor in his
community, and has less and less the role of a general
leader of thought. Dr. John C. H. Wu comments:

 . . . the profession of law is not a mere craft for
making a living, as the layman is inclined to think—
perhaps not without a certain justification, when he
observes the narrow intellectual interests of the lawyers he may happen to know. As Justice Holmes testi-
fied, "One heard Burke saying that law sharpens the

mind by narrowing it. One heard in Thackeray of a
lawyer bending all the powers of a great mind to a
mean profession. One saw that artists and poets
shrank from it as from an alien world. One doubted
oneself how it could be worthy of the interest of an
intelligent mind."[2]

This is of course an overstatement, but it is becoming
more and more accurate. Today lawyers tend to know
more and more about less and less, due to the increasing
compartmentalization of practice.

3. Due to the increasing identification of attorneys, especially those associated with large law firms, with a variety of financial and industrial interests that have a stake
in political issues, the outcome of which will be decisions
that are good for one client and not for another, there is
much more reticence to become involved in public affairs.
More and more it is thought by the lawyer to be safer
to be silent and uninvolved. In one large West Coast law
firm all the partners and associates were advised, urged,
indeed almost directed to take no position whatsoever on
any candidate or on any of the propositions on the forth-
coming state ballot. Considering the talent available in
this particular firm, this represented the removal of a con-
siderable number of opinion makers of high potential
from the process of public decision-making—quite a contrast to the days when lawyers of such caliber (or of
any caliber) were very much looked to in the shaping of
political thought within a community.

4. With the increasing complexity of law, the layman
is less and less able readily to understand what the law-

[2] *Fountain of Justice* (New York: Sheed & Ward, 1955), page 4.

yer is about. Thus there is engendered the suspicion that
fishy things are going on. Connected with this is an increase in the conspicuousness of crime (I hesitate to say
whether or not there is a national increase in crime or an
increase in the detection of the same—this same problem
arises in a number of fields of knowledge) and in the
number of offenses, especially in the economic field; and
the inevitable identification of lawyers with this widened
variety of criminal matters increases confusion among the
people at large as to the role of attorneys in the whole
business. The fact is that there is a thin line between, on
the one hand, legitimate counseling and proper defense
of criminal defendants, and, on the other, aiding and
abetting crime. Since this is a difficult line for attorneys
to draw, it should not surprise us that the public—often
equipped only with scant newspaper reports—also finds it
a hard line to draw.

In a 45,000-word opinion, in a suit by truckers against
certain railroads, Judge Thomas J. Clary said:

> This was a carefully calculated plan under the
> guidance of confident legal counsel which sought to
> use a means of injuring and, if possible, destroying
> interstate trucking competition that would afford the
> greatest amount of constitutional protection and
> thereby seek to render it immune from the anti-trust
> laws. The further inference to be drawn is that the
> plan was to be cast in the guise of a gigantic legis-
> lative campaign in order to attempt to surround it
> with the protection of the right to assemble, the right
> to petition the legislature and freedom of speech.
> . . . The chief device used by the railroads and to a

lesser extent by the truckers, which latter did not involve violation of the Sherman and Clayton Anti-Trust Acts is one known to political experts under the terms "the big lie."[3]

Here is an instance where legal practice—at least in the mind of this particular Federal judge—slopped over the line between counseling and collaboration with evil.

5. The progress in the development of codes of legal ethics—good things in themselves—have tended to encourage the notion that the minimum is the maximum of the lawyer's responsibility.

We should pause here for a moment and seek to analyze the role of such codes in the whole picture. All through the history of religion the same problem has existed. In the Old Testament it is represented by the tension between the priest and the prophet. The priest is good at drawing up sets of rules that can give people a reliable basis for ordinary behavior; he tries to cover—well or ill—all of the standard situations. Then along comes the prophet, who generally overstates the case, and says in effect, "These rules are no good at all." For example, "Incense is an abomination to me"[4] (when the same Scriptures say, "Let my prayer be set forth in thy sight as the incense"[5]) or "Thinkest thou that I will eat bulls' flesh, and drink the blood of goats?"[6] (when the same Scriptures set forth detailed rules for animal sacrifice[7]). Actually what the prophet is trying to say with

---

[3] Quoted in Rothschild, *op. cit.*
[4] Isaiah 1:13.
[5] Psalm 141:2.
[6] Psalm 50:13.
[7] See the Pentateuch, *passim.*

emphasis is: "God wants more than such things as these." This is what Jesus, as prophet, meant when He said, "Unless your righteousness exceeds that of the scribes and Pharisees, you will never enter the kingdom of heaven."[8] Then the prophet points out obligations that are not covered by the rulebooks and that the people are not fulfilling. What the prophet really wants is for the conscience to operate in the undefined areas, with the intuition of the heart, not merely following the work of a technical legal mind directed toward the exegesis of existing codified rules.

So the next generation of priests get to work and jack up the codes. They cover in detail more areas of decent behavior in human relationships. Now the priests feel that things are all set. The people are given the impression that if they can match up with all these rules—now increased in number and scope—they are safe from moral censure from God or from man. Most any of us would feel kindly disposed toward such an approach. It would be nice to believe that if we can check off a given set of rules then we can relax and avoid making moral decisions about complex issues as they arise on an *ad hoc* basis, avoid the necessity of making great big difficult decisions in the gray areas. This is the attraction of what we might call in this country "suburban ethics": "I pay my taxes, mend my fences, don't kick my neighbor's dog, don't butt into other people's business, and don't talk religion: I'm a good guy."

Then the next generation of prophets repeats the proc-

[8] Matthew 5:20.

ess; then the next generation of priests responds as before. Actually one can make a "geological" study of the
Old Testament in terms of the strata of material that has
accumulated by this process of the swing of the pendu-
lum between priest and prophet. And the strata—hun-
dreds of years apart—often appear within the same book
of the Old Testament.

Moving into the first century A.D., we find that this was
in essence the quarrel between Jesus and the Pharisees.
Jesus respected the codes. "Think not that I have come to
abolish the law and the prophets; I have come not to
abolish them but to fulfill them."[9] At the same time he
bore the role of the prophet in relation to an oversimplified codification of morality. The Jewish law was
highly developed indeed, and more so than that of any
other group up to that time; yet, in the nature of things, it
could not cover the *ad hoc* problems of human relationship as to which persons should not relax but rather feel a
sense of conscience, indeed of uneasiness, particularly in
the face of the paradoxical nature of the many decisions
to be made in this realm, as contrasted with more obvious
situations subject to codification. This was the quarrel between Saint Augustine of Hippo and Pelagius of Britain.
The issue came up conspicuously in the Reformation in
the issue of justification by grace and works versus justification by grace through faith, and the question of the existence of works of supererogation.[10] Again we see the
problem reasserted by latter-day prophets such as Søren

[9] Matthew 5:17.
[10] See my *Doing the Truth* (Garden City, N.Y.: Doubleday &
Company, 1955), Chapter VIII.

Kierkegaard, Karl Barth, Emil Brunner, Reinhold Niebuhr, A. T. Mollegen and Paul Tillich.

It is in this more pervasive context that we can see the relevance of the problem of the codes of legal ethics and the ethics beyond legal ethics. Obvious, obtuse forms of undesirable professional behavior can readily be covered by these codes. They can certainly establish a standard pattern of attorney–client, attorney–attorney and attorney–court relationships. And this is very valuable indeed, just as in the case of morality in general. Take the Ten Commandments. They give us a very good rule of thumb as to standard situations, thus saving us from the necessity of going through a great moral struggle of repeated contextual patterns. For example, I happen to be an administrator of an ecclesiastical jurisdiction in a very rapidly growing area. With virtually no endowments, with almost one mission church mounted on the back of every established parish, there is a constant need of funds. Suppose when visiting one of the parish churches I see as I offer the alms at the altar a twenty-dollar bill. In terms of the ultimate meaning of things, it may well be that the twenty dollars could better be used in one of our new growing places, and if there were time during the singing of the Doxology I might well debate the pros and cons, perhaps even decide to slip the twenty-dollar bill up the sleeve of my rochet. But it is much simpler, and in terms of the general reliability of things, wiser, to recall the simple commandment, "Thou shalt not steal." We can even reduce this to a less traditional level and come out with about the same answer: one could perhaps make a better case for green being the proper color for stop and red the proper color for go, but it is better for all-round reliability simply to follow the mores and stop on red and go on green, with proper attention to amber in the meanwhile.

So these things have a value. But such rules, whether they be traffic regulations or commandments from Mount Sinai, do not exhaust the full moral dimension of things. In fact, it should be pointed out that because of the necessary generalization of such rules they are pregnable to the assault of a higher claim.

. . ."Thou shalt not commit adultery" is one of the commandments and is regarded as a fundamental norm, yet the heroine of the apocryphal book of Judith goes forth from besieged Jerusalem to the camp of the Assyrian commander Holofernes prepared to lie with him that she may have the opportunity of slaying him and thus freeing her nation. (The fact that his intemperance as to the proffered refreshments happily relieved her of the necessity of committing adultery in order to relieve him of his head does not change the moral character of her prior decision.) Judith could have avoided the burden of undertaking this hazardous enterprise simply by reciting the commandments. But the tradition of her nobility rests upon the fact that she did not. To her conscience the saving of the people of God from the pagan invader inspired in her a vocation to act in this unconventional manner. Yet the commandment was not thereafter rewritten (to, for example, "Thou shall not commit adultery except to raise the siege of a city"), nor would anyone argue that the adultery or the slaying—as such—would be a good thing. Yet she remains a heroine. Her judgment about her vocation transcended the law—even so hallowed a law as the one against illicit sexual experience and the one against killing. Decisions not unlike hers were made during the last World War by members of the French Underground, whose deeds in service of the hopes of freedom have evoked praise, not condemnation, from quite moral people.[11]

This is said not to debunk the Ten Commandments or, by analogy, the codes of legal ethics, but simply to put them in their proper place. They are fine for standard situations; they by no means relate successfully to major moral struggles in regard to complexities that elude easy categorization and are not readily definable. There is something more here, something bigger, and it is this something more that we are seeking to grasp in this book.

Now because it has been this tendency through all history to rate that which is meant to be the minimum as the maximum, because people like to relax, with no special or unique problems to wrestle, there is the negative effect of codes of legal ethics. They ought to be there, but we must keep stirring the sense of conscience to make clear that they represent the least, not the most, of which is to be expected from the members of our profession.

These factors that have been outlined are a mixed bag. Some of them could not possibly be helped, in the nature of things. Others reflect critically and rather specifically on the way we have been looking at things or doing them. The list of factors point to two things. First, there is something wrong with the public image of the lawyer. I am

[11] *Doing the Truth,* pages 56–57.

afraid that it also shows that there is something wrong with the reality that helps create the image. In short, part of the solution is a matter of public relations: better education of the public—the laymen—as to the meaning and role of this profession of ours. A lot of this is going on, and it is good—for example, the development of Law Day throughout the country under the auspices of the American Bar Association. But at the same time it requires a deeper understanding on the part of attorneys themselves as to the scope and depth of their commitment.

III

The Lawyer's Profession and Vocation

In the classification of jobs, we tend to think of profession as higher than vocation. We rate a professional school above a vocational school. But rather elementary etymological study will show that the word "vocation" is the nobler of the two words. "Profession" comes from a Latin root that enables us to define the word as "what you hold yourself out to be." The Latin root of "vocation" leads us to this meaning: "What you are called to be." Now to be in a profession without a sense of vocation would seem to imply that there is no higher claim upon you than what the lineaments of your particular specialty will require of you by way of public expectation. For example, the innkeeper's situation (increasingly challenging in Georgia, or for that matter in some hotels in the North): if you call your outfit an inn (or these days, a hotel or motel) you have committed yourself to take all comers, simply because you have professed yourself to be an innkeeper. If you hold yourself forth as a lawyer, then you have not necessarily committed yourself professionally to more than following the rules of the game: the canons of legal ethics, the statutes, the case law as developed by precedent—being the stereotyped decent mechanic of a given portion of the machinery of life. It would be expected that there would be no irregularity in your behavior. It would be assumed that you would be reliable in performing your paid-for services in a well-defined area of responsibility.

I think there is at least one more dimension to the word, one that helps makes the transition between this word and that of "vocation."

First, in order to be what you hold yourself out to be, you have to be properly prepared in your particular case or in regard to the particular matter in which you serve as a consultant. This means specific and specialized study, with concentration, and not simply playing by ear.

More than that, this means a continuing study to enable you to be broadly prepared in the fields in which you practice. This includes relevant opinions, of course, law review articles, periodic new material for loose-leaf services, and cognate literature (often of an extralegal nature). This all goes toward maintaining a general grasp that enables you to bring a good degree of imagination to any given case that might be brought to you. This is quite a different matter than simply doing research on a particular case. Constant study of a given field better enables you, in relation to a particular case, to know what to look for in terms of specific research. There is at least this much involved in the minimum responsibility even of lawyers who would regard no higher claim upon them than that implied in the word "profession."

Here we can profit from a story from another field. An adult conference was scheduled in one of the Episcopal dioceses. The teaching staff consisted of members of the faculty of a seminary in the same state. They headed for the conference by way of a direct but difficult road, and en route their car broke down. As they started to walk some miles along the muddy road to the nearest town, one of them, who was Professor of Christian Ethics, said to the others, "I hope the mechanic we find in the next town is a Christian, but even more, I hope he is a good mechanic."[1] First things first.

Great preachers or great teachers are persons who are involved in a wider preparation than is required for a particular occasion. And this is true of great lawyers. When Joseph Story was inaugurated Dane Professor of Law in Harvard University in 1829, he said:

> Many of our most illustrious statesmen have been lawyers; but they have been lawyers liberalized by philosophy, and a large intercourse with the wisdom of ancient and modern times. The perfect lawyer, like the perfect orator, must accomplish himself for his duties by familiarity with every study. It may truly be said, that to him nothing, that concerns human nature or human art, is indifferent and useless. He should search the human heart, and explore to their sources the passions, and appetites, and feelings of mankind. . . . He should for this purpose make the masterspirits of all ages pay contribution to his labors. He should walk abroad through nature, and

[1] Attributed to the Rev. Professor A. T. Mollegen of Virginia Theological Seminary.

elevate his thoughts, and warm his virtues, by a contemplation of her beauty, and magnificence, and harmony. He should examine well the precepts of religion, as the only solid basis of civil society; and gather from them, not only his duty, but his hopes; not merely his consolations, but his discipline and his glory.[2]

And then Mr. Justice Holmes, who is a bit more cautious about endorsing things specifically religious, nevertheless went this far:

Happiness, I am sure from having known many successful men, cannot be won simply by being counsel for great corporations and having an income of fifty thousand dollars. An intellect great enough to win the prize needs other food besides success. The remoter and more general aspects of the law are those which give it universal interest. It is through them that you not only become a great master in your calling, but connect your subject with the universe and catch an echo of the infinite, a glimpse of its unfathomable process, a hint of the universal law.[3]

Now, quite easily, after these quotations, we turn to the second word, "vocation." It is based simply on the participle of *voco: vocatus*, meaning "having been called."

[2] *Miscellaneous Writings* (Boston: James Munroe & Company, 1835, page 460).
[3] Quoted in *Report of the Joint Conference on Professional Responsibility of the Association of American Law Schools and American Bar Association* (St. Paul, Minn.: West Publishing Company), page 16.

Since it is grammatically in the passive voice, the question is obviously raised: by whom? The word requires the ablative of agent. One way to get at the problem is to translate it into the active voice: *voco*—"I call." Here we have shown the subject. And the subject is something outside the object. The word "profession" works from the inside out, but the word "vocation" only works from the outside in. One of the Hebrew words for "work" is *melacha*. But the archaic meaning of this Hebrew word is "an angel sent of God." This symbolizes the fact that in the Biblical tradition a calling in any realm is a call from God. It is a word to us to get with it. This provides no specific directive to man to serve in any particular calling or profession, but it makes clear that our role is to take our part, according to our particular talents and limitations, in the total work of the world.

The reason why I feel fairly secure both in being stamped with an ecclesiastical character and being an existentialist both in jurisprudence (not being particularly allied with natural law) and in ethics generally, is the fact that I believe there is one great Commandment, the ancient *Shema Yisrael*. It has been used in Jewish worship, publicly or in the home, for several thousand years and it is used in Anglican services at every Eucharist: "Hear O Israel, the Lord thy God is One. And thou shalt love the Lord thy God with thy whole heart, thy whole mind and thy whole strength."[4]

[4] In the Episcopal Church in the United States, the "copyright" is somewhat violated; we leave out the first sentence, introducing the second by "Hear what our Lord Jesus Christ saith," when actually Jesus did not invent this but learned it at his mother's knee.

Now the first sentence ties very logically to the second. Here we see the ultimate connection between religion and ethics. That is why "whole" is used as the adjective. There is only One of Him; hence he is entitled to all— all of each of us. This injunction is in contrast to the ethics of the surrounding polytheisms of the Middle East in the current Mediterranean world.

We must remember that the ancient "gods" of the ancient world do not represent nonsense or mere superstition. They represent foci of human aspiration—of purposes generally good. Today we don't build sanctuaries to such gods or erect statues in their honor or burn incense before them, but various human beings are motivated by one or more of the aspirations that these gods represented. For example, the Baalim of the Canaanite culture stood for fertility: more flocks, more crops, more people to harvest the crops and tend the flocks. No, we don't worship Baal: we call it Production—and many are its worshipers. Other names are suggestive: Ceres—cereal and grain is a dominating focus of some people's life and work; Venus —the mention of the name is enough to make the point; the same is true of Mammon; Mars has his place with those who even in our perilous nuclear situation remain jingoists; Apollo—many, fortunately, put a high premium on intellectual excellence.

There's nothing wrong with some of these gods, provided there is one overall total claim upon us that can keep them in subordination, can keep our various foci in proportion. In a familiar canticle we refer to "a great King above all gods."[5] Thus even in a monotheistic re-

5 *Venite, exultemus Domino* (Psalm 95).

ligion we recognize the place of the specialized gods—
under the sovereignty of the one true God.

This latter recognition is very important. These are not
lectures on mental health, but it should be noted in passing that all this has a bearing on one's stability and in-
tegration.[6] The trouble with monolatry—the worship of a
single false god—is that the god, having feet of clay, lets
one down, with inevitably resulting cynicism, frustration,
or even despair. When one's god dies, sometimes the wor-
shiper dies with it. And the trouble with polytheism (a
number of foci unregulated by an overarching meaning)
is that polytheism in worship leads to schizophrenia in
life. One is torn every which way. The secret of inte-
gration is that there is one big claim over all the little
claims. Søren Kierkegaard has reminded us that "purity
of heart is to will one thing." And he defines true religion
as "an absolute relationship to the Absolute and a relative
relationship to all else."

Now if there be such an Absolute, He has a claim on
all of a person, and therefore the totality of one's being is
involved and not simply his lawyerness or his sociality,
etc. It is the whole man that is under claim, at all moments and in all relationships. A lawyer could not be
exempted from this even if a canon of legal ethic or a
statute—or even a constitution—explicitly provided that
no more than what is explicitly specified shall be required
of any attorney. That would not exempt him from the
total claim, if there be such a claim.

We cannot here consider the problem in terms of all

[6] See further my *Beyond Anxiety* (New York: Charles Scribner's
Sons, 1953), Chapter I.

the world's various religious systems; hence I will have to be content to work it through in terms of the Judeo-Christian tradition.

What kind of a Claimant is this? This is important to know, because we are told right in the beginning of Genesis that we are made in the image of God, and therefore how we are to live and what we are to be doing is determined by what we think He is like and what He is doing. For example, Genesis tells us that He is turning chaos into order. Obviously that work isn't complete; the world is still quite a mess, not only in the physical universe, but in human relationships. Hence we are called to help finish that job: we are called to be co-orderers with God, to help tidy things up. Of course, since we are free, we can turn back into chaos such order as there already is in given situations. In fact, we are now so scientifically clever we are capable of turning the whole thing back into chaos. That would be quite a joke on God; He'd have to start all over with this earth.

The task of man is to use his special peculiar talents in this ordering process. (And everyone is peculiar, and meant to be. Here there are no civil service classifications. Everyone is engaged as a specialist.)

God is not only Creator and Orderer; He is Redeemer. And so man is called to be redemptive. This work is not finished either. There are plenty of sick people, sad people, wounded people, frustrated people, and we are called to help God in the process of their healing.

God is also Holy Spirit, that is, holy *esprit de corps*—builder and inspirer of community. So we are called to help build community among men—a task by no means complete. But, as the Nicene Creed asserts, this same

Holy Spirit "spake through the prophets." Thus we also are called to be judges and reformers of community, of our common life.[7]

In these ways, as made in the image of God, each of us is called to share in putting things right. This is fundamentally what gives work importance. A given piece of constructive work has eternal significance because it is part of the whole ongoing process of the creation, the redemption, and the community-building of the world. Another way of putting it is that we are all called to the ministry. (This is echoed in some codes of legal ethics, which refer to the Law of which we are "ministers.") Those of us who wear our collars backward are not the whole ministry. We are simply engaged in one of the specialized aspects of the whole ministry to which all men are called.

Granted this fundamental postulate, it is not surprising that the Scriptures—Old and New Testaments alike— stress the dignity of work. However, built right in is a warning against work idolatry. This is what lies behind the meaning of the Sabbath. It says, in effect, "Knock it off; work isn't all there is." In making this point Bishop Richard S. M. Emrich says:

> Holy Scripture does not only teach the dignity of work; it also warns against work idolatry. We can see the meaning of the ancient teaching of the Sabbath if we will consider a present problem. Not only are there people who want to avoid work because they do not see its meaning—there are also what Brunner calls "work fanatics," men who look upon work as an

[7] See Chapter VI.

end in itself, who have forgotten how to play, rest, or live. Work is for them an idol that possesses them. They do not have work: work has them. It is obvious that there is an inhuman quality in men who cannot rest or play. Their work fanaticism, says Brunner, is a revelation of the poverty of their souls. The double problem of the loss of a will to work . . . and of a work fanaticism comes from the same source—the loss of the eternal meaning of our lives.

The limits which must be placed upon work lest it become a demoniac end in itself, destroying life, are revealed in Scripture in the Sabbath commandment. We are not made for work: we are made for God, and are meant to serve Him in all we do. If the chief end of man is work, and work alone integrates human life, then at retirement man will disintegrate as he loses his chief end. All things on earth have meaning—the trouble is they do not have enough meaning. When we see that our true purpose in life is to serve God and enjoy Him forever, we will work even if necessity does not drive us, and quietly care for our souls in worship and recreation because that too —the rhythm of life—is God's will. . . .[8]

The author cites the parable of the entrepreneur who planned bigger barns for his increasing goods and produce, ending with the words, "But God said to him, 'Fool! This night your soul is required of you.'"[9] This is

[8] "The Church and Work" in *Man at Work in God's World*, edited by George E. DeMille (New York: Longmans, Green & Co., 1956), pages 54–55.
[9] Luke 12:20–21; *cf.* Ecclesiastes 2:18–19.

the other side of the coin. There is a holiness, a dignity, a calling to work, giving it an eternal meaning, but we are in peril if we idolize work and make it the sole end of our existence.

All through history there has been vacillation with regard to the status and role of work. In primitive cultures, work—at first grazing and then agriculture—was actually an integral part of religion, geared to the cycle of holy seasons and liturgical observances. We have remnants of that in Rogationtide, the English Harvest Festival, and the American Thanksgiving Day. But with the coming of civilization—we see it particularly in the Greco-Roman civilization—there was a deconsecration of work. The ideal of life became that of the *rentier,* the man who lives off the work of others. Such was the person in society who was really respected, really important.

The first subsequent attempt to provide a solid basis of respect for work was the Benedictine movement. We cannot go into the whole philosophy of St. Benedict's Rule and its implications for societal attitudes, but there we see the revival of the sense of the value of being at work, its beauty and satisfactions and its holiness as related to the perfection of the universe. As the philosopher of history, Arnold J. Toynbee, points out, people who get that idea work very effectively and hence tend to become successful.[10] Using a system analogous to a corporation or trust setup, the monks who started out to do good did well (to borrow a phrase that has been applied to some

---

[10] I rely on Toynbee in this whole analysis. See his "Man at Work in the Light of History" in *Man at Work in God's World, ibid.,* pages 3–41.

of the missionary families who went to Hawaii). The monks, under a vow of poverty, as they expanded their lands and increased the development of the same, fared more and more comfortably. Thus as we get deeper into the Middle Ages, the basic motif begins to disappear. Those not in on the system figure out ways to get in. With this end in mind (the control and expansion of property) quite undedicated persons (often determined to keep one foot in the world) decided to be monks, particularly if, blessed with good connections, they might hope to become abbots soon. In the end, others decided to take a shortcut (typified by Henry VIII).[11]

In his analysis Toynbee moves directly to the Puritan movement. But, on the way, we should pause a moment at the Reformation. The relationship of Calvinism to the rise of capitalism has been too fully treated to occupy us here, but it has not been frequently enough noted that Martin Luther as well as John Calvin in the abolition of the religious orders did not intend to downgrade the religious life but to exalt a sense of vocation of all members of society. It is true, however, that the Puritan movement put a special stress on the value and significance of work. The result was a repeat of the outcome of the Benedictine movement. The fruitage was highly successful. When work results in success, it becomes increasingly viewed as a means thereto. Success replaces a sense of vocation as the motive and work loses its holiness and be-

[11] As to Henry's dissolution of the monasteries there are two sides, and here I express my Anglican bias. By that time fewer and fewer monks operated larger and larger properties; on the other hand, one cannot give this well-known king very many points for high motivation. In other words, it was the shortcut.

comes once more secularized, and deconsecrated. All this had to do with the ultimate question not only of these chapters, but of life. It is within this framework that we shall deal in the subsequent lectures with the particular roles of the lawyer's vocation.

A good question at this point is, What difference does it make? What difference does all this make in what one really will do in the exercise of his profession? Why ponder these troublesome things? It is true that such reflections might cause some lawyers loss of sleep and some daytime torment of conscience—all easily avoided by the presupposition of the distinguished lawyer I quoted in the first chapter, "There is no question."

There is a difference. In fact there are at least three differences:

1. It leads to more responsible decision-making, for example, as to what you will and will not do within the limited time you have at the office and out of the office. There is no religious or ethical system that, when consciously analyzed, would absolve a lawyer from responsibility as to such decision-making. That is why in the next chapter we shall be considering the role of the lawyer as judge. Here we shall not be thinking especially of the judicial office whether by election or appointment, but of the role every practicing lawyer plays right in his office in connection with the various matters brought to his attention. Important all through is his priority scale and his effect on persons. This means decision after decision, and in deciding, the broader the base of responsibility the better.

2. This approach can debunk certain illusions. A sound religious orientation maturely and consciously held in re-

lationship to one's life as a lawyer—as distinguished from piety and church activity in the narrower sense—can be illuminating here. First of all, we will more readily perceive that there are no easy answers, no utopian possibilities or easy remedies for the problems with which we are confronted. To quote Bishop Emrich again, "We reject utopian illusions, and know that, while earth can be improved and brought closer to God's will, earth will never be heaven. As Christians we know not only the sovereign will of God for man, but we also have an insight into the depths of human existence which saves us both from a belief in superficial remedies and from quick discouragement."[12]

Also, we will be saved from illusions about ourselves. The Biblical faith constantly reminds us that we are creatures and therefore finite. We are limited. This should save us from being too sure about things. It may be effective courtroom technique to be absolutely sure about one's cause, absolutely confident of the erroneous basis of the opposing counsel's position—not so much with judges, I might say, as with juries. However, effective though this may be as apologetics or forensics, let not the lawyer himself be taken in by this show of absolutes. He will be a more thoughtful and perceptive lawyer and, incidentally, more ready on rebuttal if he has not actually been all that sure, if he has not oversimplified things. This may lead him to listen sometimes and to be more open to the insights from other lives than his own.

Finally, an adherent to the Biblical faith should have

[12] "The Church and Work" in *Man at Work in God's World*, page 62.

no illusions about his own virtue. He should know that even when he is at his best his decision-making and motivation "are always tainted with corruption, and this saves him from the fanaticism which will not permit criticism or free discussion."[13] Important is the conscious recognition of one's mixed motives even in that which would seem to work for good. Bishop Emrich provides a useful analogy from Communism. There is much evil in Communism, but for that matter there is much evil within ourselves and in the practical operation of the free enterprise system. As he points out, "the worst aspect of Communism is its awful self-righteousness, as revealed in the invective hurled at any opponent. Self-righteousness is blindness and leads to cruelty. The knowledge of our own sins, of our own need for forgiveness, quiets our proud hearts, and gives that atmosphere in which free discussion and criticism are possible."[14] Such an approach will modify simple distinctions between the good guys and the bad guys.

3. The third difference is this: a consistent religio-ethical outlook provides for value judgments a point of reference outside the system. To continue with the Judeo-Christian approach, we affirm the reality of the Kingdom of God not simply in terms of Heaven ahead, but in terms of another dimension of life, loyalty and power now. To summarize two sayings of Saint Paul, we are citizens of the Kingdom of God and colonists here.[15] Thus we

[13] *Ibid.*
[14] *Ibid.*
[15] Ephesians 2:19; Philippians 3:20 (James Moffatt's translation: "But we are a colony of heaven, . . .).

live in two worlds. This is no escapism; indeed, it strengthens the challenge in one's earthly calling. The colonist is always trying to make where he is look like his home country. The citizen of the Kingdom of God is eager that life here and now be conformed more and more to what Saint Thomas Aquinas has called "our true native land."[16] (This is the only kind of colonialism I am willing to endorse.) We gain our norms not from the mores, not from what is accepted, not from what "They say," not from what is safe, but from the standards of the Kingdom— what is perceived to be the Will of God for His world. "Do not be conformed to this world," Saint Paul enjoins us, "but be transformed by the renewal of your mind, that you may prove what is the will of God, what is good and acceptable and perfect."[17]

Attorneys-at-law who grasp this note of the Great Tradition will join "the goodly fellowship of the Prophets,"[18] the critics of the status quo, the reformers of the Law itself.

So whether a given religion is true or not, it does make a difference in the practice of a profession, even one so apparently self-sufficient as the legal profession.

[16] In *O salutaris hostia,* The [Episcopal] Hymnal, 1948, Hymn 209.
[17] Romans 12:2.
[18] *Te Deum laudamus,* The Book of Common Prayer, page 10.

IV

The Lawyer as Judge

In Anglo-Saxon jurisprudence there is an ambiguity about the judicial role of the lawyer. On the one hand, there is a sharp distinction between the role of the judge and legal counsel. Under the adversary system the former is supposed to be totally objective (and if he proves obtusely unobjective, he is removed by impeachment, trial or failure of reappointment or re-election), while the latter is expected to be partisan. But there are limits to the partisanship of counsel for the parties, as is indicated by the role of any lawyer in a case as an officer of the Court. He, too, has a primary claim upon him in the overall enterprise of the pursuit of justice. Yet, it is expected that the emphasis in his preparation and presentation of the case will be upon the good points in favor of his party and upon the mitigation of the effect upon judge and/or jury of good points developed by opposing counsel.

From any ultimate philosophical or ethical point of

view, this biased role is hard to justify, but pragmatically it has over the centuries worked out very well. More facts are brought clearly to light before the deciding authority by the respective partisans than would be the case without them. Hence, in the end, better justice is done. This experienced reality is recognized by the fact that the State (in the case of public defenders) or the Court (in terms of appointment of a particular counsel—in practice with, but in theory even without, their consent) or voluntary agencies (principally legal aid clinics) provide legal counsel thenceforth to be motivated by partisan commitment. Part of the good result arises from the role in which, under the system, the lawyer is placed. There is almost an automatic frame of mind that gives him a certain style in the shaping up of a given side of the case. Part of it is the fruit of Original Sin. The will to win is one of the manifestations of the self-centering tendency in man, and it manifests itself in legal practice even when a fee is not involved, for example, in the zeal of an attorney appointed by the Court to defend without fee a defendant charged with a crime. Original Sin is sufficiently powerful for us so that when the factor of a fee is added it is likely that there will be even greater zeal. But, nevertheless, zeal is not necessarily lacking when the prospect of a fee is.

Paradoxically enough, it is before a man reaches the Court—right in the attorney's office—that the lawyer appears most fully in the role as an officer of the Court. In the *courtroom* this somewhat ceremonial phrase represents a prohibition against certain excesses; the *office* represents a mandate for a positive role. It is here that the lawyer is really acting as judge, as a deal is put together or as things are sorted out in connection with the decision to undertake, or to defend against, possible litigation.

In a measure any lawyer, with or without a conscious sense of overall vocation, exercises this role. It is much better if he exercises it consciously. It is in his office that he should regard the chair at his desk as a seat of justice. It is here that he should sit down each morning with a sense of solemnity (albeit without announcing "Oyez") as an officer of the Court, now viewing the phrase not merely as a restriction on his temptation to muck up the judicial process, but rather as a challenge to serve as a magistrate-in-the-first-instance. If practicing lawyers by and large consciously assumed this role, society as a whole would be much better off, our Court calendars would be much clearer—freeing judicial time to be better focused on more seriously litigable matters, and more practical justice would be achieved and much expense avoided for all concerned. Once things get going, of course, the lawyer is an agent of his client. But it is important that there be a preliminary stage in which the lawyer is on a level removed from his client, sensitive to the latter's personal needs (see the next chapter), yet judging the client's situation in the magisterial role.

Right here we must state that there are limits to this role. Unlike a judge, he cannot, in the last analysis, tell a client what or what not to do. In the first place, he *cannot*, because there are other lawyers available. The client need only go down the hall in the same building, or turn to the yellow pages of the phone book. But, second, he *ought* not to. He is not called upon to run the client's life. Yet there is an in-between role that is more than a judgment as to what might go in the courts, what

might be a contract that will bind, what might be a deal
that will hold together; namely, an ethical judgment as
to whether it will be a good thing. The degree to which
the attorney can exercise the latter part of this role depends upon the sustained character of the relationship,
the degree of trust the client has been able to place in
him and, ultimately, what kind of person the lawyer himself is.

There is another aspect to the judicial role of the attorney in his office that is entirely in the attorney's hands,
without appeal. If there is a final claim on the attorney
along the lines I suggested in the previous chapter, then
obviously he will not take every case that comes in the
office. He will not need to aid and abet everything proposed to him. Here I am not talking about those things
he cannot do because of the prohibitions of the canons
of legal ethics (ambulance chasing, double agency,
etc.). We are now talking about the dimension beyond
arrest or disbarment, namely, the effect on his choices
that comes from his total perspective, his world view. The
standard canons of legal ethics respect this privilege of
choice on the part of the attorney. This provides there is
nothing wrong in defending anybody or acting for anyone, but the canons also make clear that an attorney
need take no case he doesn't want to take. (Very similar
is the canon law in my particular tradition. I can, as
Bishop, with the aid of a matrimonial court, act as judge
on the basis of a sheaf of papers and say to the given
person that he may be remarried in the Church.[1] But
any priest in my diocese who does not agree with my

[1] Canons of the Episcopal Church, Canon 18, § 2.

judgment or does not feel that the new marriage will be
a sound one, need not marry the couple.[2] In short, the
canons of legal ethics say that you can take any case,
and then say that you need not take any case—whether
because of preoccupation with other matters, laziness
(the fishing may be good in your parts at this point), or
moral discrimination.

This freedom of discrimination guaranteed, open then
is the question, What kind of potential court case, or
what kind of deal, will you be involved in? We can rather
quickly exclude certain possibilities.

After hearing a story, you see your client wronged. The
clear case plus the bold grievance. Your client has lost
his shirt in a really dirty transaction. Or your client has
inspired you with his courage. For example, he is a Freedom Rider and he suffered in jail, knowing, as you do,
that the law under which he was jailed eventually will
be declared unconstitutional by the U. S. Supreme Court
—and would have been by now, except for the intolerable
delays in our Federal judicial machinery. You get with
it; your emotions are stirred. The fee is helpful, but regardless you want to see the wrong righted. Here you are
really an Advocate. You want to smash evil, whether it
be a bad state law or those persons you conceive to be
evilly motivated. You want to be in there slugging. Here
the situation is clear. The whole person—the whole moral
person—is drawn into action.

Then, there are the routine cases where the matter of
legal rights are so clear that there are no exciting issues

[2] *Ibid.*, Canon 17, § 4.

presented, and the lawyer acts without moral question, simply in his general role of tidying things up. This sort of thing he does with his left hand.

And then there is the clear case minus. For example, the apparent role of attorneys referred to in the railroad-trucking case cited earlier.[3] If counsel were asked to enter into a scheme to use a suit in a court of law simply as a public relations springboard, such a lawyer who would let himself be a party to such a scheme of distortion would deserve the rebuke that the Federal judge's opinion delivered—in short, "the big lie." A second example pointed out by Rothschild,[4] is the lawyer who becomes the regular adviser to the editors of scandal magazines. He is put in the role of determining how the magazine can produce the maximum of scandal with a minimum of risk from libel suits. This kind of lawyer has really gone into the editorial business, seeking to draw a thin line that will give the greatest possible scope to a deleterious enterprise. These last two examples are illustrations of many that easily come to mind and that certainly should not present a great moral struggle to any lawyer of integrity or, one should say, to any person of integrity. Decent people simply would not want to be a part of any such thing.

Hence the clear case plus and the clear case minus need not detain us. But there are many situations that are not on these two edges, but rather fall somewhere in the middle. Here is where our problem lies.

[3] See page 10.
[4] *Op. cit.*, page 6.

First, let's take an example of a proposal that has a good object but where the methods to be used are marginal. Let us assume the attorney is confident that the objective sought by the client is wise, sound and right, but it is apparent that working it out legally will be a bit tight. For example:

1. Such an ethical question is presented when either or both of two standard pleas are technically available, namely, the Statute of Frauds and the Statute of Limitations. To narrow the question: it would seem clear that if the attorney feels quite confident that the case against his client has no merit, it is actually virtuous to plead one or the other of these two Statutes if they are applicable, since this saves everybody's time: the Court's, the plaintiff's, the defendant's, and the counsel for both. If the case has been filed too late or the alleged obligation is not in writing, then by the pleading of such defenses a benefit has been conferred on all, including the plaintiff, since presumably less of his lawyer's time will be taken up and he will be in for a smaller fee.

The harder case is when the defendant's attorney is not all that sure about his client's position on the merits; harder still is the situation where the defendant's attorney is quite sure that his client is under a genuine moral obligation to pay up or to do what he promised to do, or where it is apparent that he has imposed a real wrong on the plaintiff. There is no easy answer to this, but these are the alternative possibilities:

(1) The attorney's collaboration in the pleading of one or both of these defenses is unethical under such circumstances, and he becomes a party to the frustration of genuine human justice.

(2) In society the given rules of law, including those of procedure, are part of the fabric of expectancies. So viewed, rules of procedure—and of jurisdiction, for that matter—really are *substantive,* not just "adjective law." They are intended to serve basic purposes: they are not merely technicalities or machinery. Following this premise, one can reasonably say that an oral promise that does not meet the standards set by the Statute of Frauds is no promise, no matter what words were used nor how firmly the other party's hand was shaken—simply because the representative agencies of our society that have structured the promising function have attached no binding effect (and hence no rightful expectation of a binding effect) to promissory noises outside of the defined ways of effectuating mutual obligation.

The same reasoning can be applied to the Statute of Limitations. We do not recognize in our society that what might have been justiciable wrongs do not exist as wrongs if not pressed within a given number of years. There is good reason why such rules are made. The openness of the courts to *res gestae* hearsay statements because of their fresh relationship to the event commented upon illustrates by analogy the conviction that the nearer to the time of the event the case is tried the more likely it will be that facts are presented with a relative degree of exactitude. Hence, on the other end of the scale, there is reason why an arbitrary time limit has been set beyond which no facts can be presented at all. Memories grow dull, illusions—and delusions—can develop, witnesses become decreasingly available. The chance that the full picture will be presented becomes more and more minimal as time goes on. Thus it can be said that in terms of over-

all policy—whatever might be the countervailing circumstances in a given situation—the appropriate agents of
society have decided that a right asserted beyond a given
time is not a right at all.

This approach is particularly plausible in the case of
contract claims, the Statute of Limitations and the Statute of Frauds presumably having been taken into account
at the time of the agreement (*ignoratio legis excusat ne-
minem*)—in regard to the given right's actually not existing when the given statute is applicable. The analogy
is not so apparent in the case of torts where the injured
person is not involved one way or the other in the area of
expectancy. Yet, even here, properly advised of the law,
he should have proceeded in time—within the time that
society has deemed is a better time to try things.

The fact that more space has been given to the second
alternative than the first does not mean that I have decided for this position. I am not at all sure; but in any
case these are the alternatives for the given lawyer to
weigh conscientiously.

2. What are some of the logical and ethical considerations in the matter of dealing with a thin line between
tax avoidance and tax evasion? One answer is that it is
immoral to engage in seeking to recover ways to frustrate
the intent and purpose of the tax laws. The other answer
is: any tax structure is arbitrary anyway; and the taxing
body (whether Congress, the State Legislature, or City
Council) has every capacity to extend the tax base to situations not previously covered (as is illustrated by the
fact that tax-avoidance schemes keep increasing the
imagination of the relevant legislative bodies). And,
therefore, if the particular arrangement the lawyer de-

vises is not covered by the relevant statute then *ipso facto* it is for the time being not taxable; hence setting up such arrangements involves no moral wrong. Again, this analysis is not meant to give the answer, either to a particular situation or as to the morals of such strategy in general. It does illustrate again the type of question with which any lawyer with a relevant sense of conscience is constantly confronted.

3. What about the procedural delays? If the counsel for the defendant does not want something to come off he can certainly find a lot of ways to see that it does not come off, either at all or for a long time. All too often as far as plaintiffs are concerned, the word from the Book of Proverbs applies: "Hope deferred makes the heart sick."[5] We can say at the outset that the use of procedural delays—for whatever purpose, good or bad—automatically involves some element of wrong. It adds to the supportive base of increasing public cynicism about the judicial process itself: it tends to strengthen the popular overgeneralization in the courts that nothing seems to move on. Since a sense of confidence in the judicial system is an important element of a viable common life, there is a public hurt here involved which certainly has to be balanced in as the pros and cons are weighed in given situations. On the other hand, balanceable against the possible contribution to public disrespect for the courts there could be in a given case a genuine conviction on the part of counsel for the defendant that the plaintiff has no legitimate case. There that defense may be complicated and expensive. He may feel that by pro-

[5] Proverbs 13:12.

cedural delays he is encouraging the chance of a settle-
ment out of court—again to the benefit of both parties
and to the court itself—assuming the usual overcrowded
calendars. Again, we are simply raising the question;
there is no easy answer.

4. For the particular type of analysis we are now undertaking, divorce practice presents an especially difficult
area. On the surface at least, it would seem to be considerably less difficult for an attorney who is a member
of a religious body that sets down rules as to his role in
such cases. For example, in the case of a Roman Catholic attorney with a Roman Catholic client, "if the client
is seeking a divorce or separation illicitly [without permission of the Church], the attorney may not co-operate
by taking the case unless there is a proportionately grave
justifying reason for his co-operation."[6] In other words,
what is normally expected is that the attorney will require that the client first seek permission from the Chan-
cery of the diocese to proceed to a civil divorce. (Incidentally, the very existence of this procedure recognizes
that there are circumstances in which, under episcopal
authority, divorces are licit among Roman Catholics; and
since this permission is not limited to the single count of
adultery, it is difficult to understand the ground of the
steadfast opposition in the Roman Catholic Church in the
State of New York to the extension of grounds for divorce beyond the one ground of adultery.) Further, "this
grave reason on the part of the attorney must become

[6] The Rt. Rev. Monsignor George J. Casey, "Canon Law on Civil
Actions in Marriage Problems" (lecture before the Catholic Lawyers Guild of Chicago, 1944).

more weighty as the unlawfulness of the petition of the client mounts in the scale of sinfulness." Monsignor Casey exemplifies this application of "the principle of material co-operation": "If a client is seeking real dissolution of a valid marriage in order to remarry, the attorney cannot represent him unless there is a more serious justifying reason." What would constitute such a reason? The following answer is given: "Such a grave reason would be the necessity of giving up his profession or losing his means of livelihood if he refused to undertake the case. In practice such a justifying grave reason will never exist."

And non-Roman Catholic attorneys whose religious or ethical scruples have convinced them of the wrongness of divorce, in general or in particular types of situations, would be under a similar prohibition of conscience (even though the prohibition might not involve formal canon law, as in the case of the Roman Catholic Church) against aiding and abetting what they are convinced is sinful. Equally clear would be the answer in conscience of an attorney whose religeo-ethical system includes a positive endorsement of divorce as the best answer (that is, the least bad answer) if the marriage has really suffered a spiritual death, where there is no hope of reconciliation and where the continuance of the marriage relationship would appear to be positively damaging to the spouses and to the children. But for attorneys morally open to divorce, the case will not always seem this clear and it is these gray cases that raise the most difficult questions.

Behind all this is a more fundamental question. Should the religious or ethical attitudes of the attorney in regard to divorce, or his application of them to the particular case before him, bear on the question of his professional involvement at all? Is this not just a matter for the client's conscience? To answer yes is to simply paraphrase the lawyer I quoted earlier, "He is supposed to do what he is paid for." It is too late in these lectures to endorse the "yes" answer. It would seem clear that the attorney, as informed by his own principles, does have a conscientious role here. At the minimum, if he does not assess the possibilities of reconciliation and if he does not fulfill in a measure at least the honorable role of *defensor vinculi,* he certainly has no right to the noble title, "Officer of the Court," since (as representing society) the courts have made clear their legitimate interest in the continuity of marriage. On the other hand, as is pointed out by Isabel Drummond, ". . . it is difficult to see what interest the State can have in coercing mismated couples to maintain to outward appearances a relation which actually does not exist."[7] Equally paradoxical is the interest of the Church in the continuity of marriage. Speaking generally, the interest is positive. But pastors in most traditions finding, after careful pastoral counseling, that a real relationship cannot be kept together will positively advise divorce, not as a good solution, but as the lesser of two evils. Even with the highest degree of conscientiousness with regard to the stability of marriage, the attorney may find himself precisely in the same situation. (As to how far he should be directive or non-directive as to the client's decision in this regard we consider in the next chapter.)

[7] *Getting a Divorce* (New York: Alfred A. Knopf, 1931), page 22.

In order sharply to raise a second question, let us assume that the attorney has no moral problem in aiding in securing a divorce for his client, but that the methods required to be used are marginal. Let us take for example a situation in New York State, in which adultery is the only ground for divorce. It is not surprising that in seeking to broaden the channel of matrimonial dissolution the legal talent in the state has applied itself to fairly imaginative measures. So much so, that in support of a bill in the New York Legislature to revise the divorce laws, the Committee on Ways and Means reported:

> . . . that evidence exists of widespread fraud, collusion, perjury, and connivance which permeates matrimonial actions and proceedings of all types affecting the family unit and the marital status, instituted in the courts of this state; that the moral, social, economic and psychological well-being of the inhabitants of the state are affected thereby.[8]

It is true that if an important area of practice be permeated by dubious ways of achieving even legitimate ends, then public confidence in the whole legal system is threatened. Yet, as everywhere else, there are in the State of New York many unhappy marriages where adultery has not entered the picture, either as cause or effect. Suppose that with the highest moral discrimination, both the New York client and the New York attorney are convinced that marital dissolution should occur. Let's assume, too, to simplify the problem, that the other spouse and attorney agree. What should they do?

[8] Excerpt from Report of Committee on Ways and Means, New York State Assembly, 1955, on proposed Bill 1026.

Several outs have been devised:

(1) *"Phony" residence.* Here it is discreetly arranged that one of the parties departs for one of the more lenient states—lenient both as to grounds of divorce and as to length of time to establish residence. (Generally it is the wife, since she usually has more free time, and because since somebody has to subsidize the expedition the breadwinner has to keep working.) Thus fraud is built into the arrangement, in one sense: there is no intent to change residence and to answer the standard question of the foreign court as to intention to settle there, there is a quick affirmance of that which in no way corresponds to the true situation. Yet, in another way, it is not fraud: nobody is fooled. It is certainly not fraud upon the court, since by virtue of the whole pattern, the court is actually part of the fraud. In short, no judge is deceived; no one intends to deceive anyone, and no one does. One difficulty with this solution is that it is expensive; not everyone can afford a six-week vacation in Reno, including the inevitable loss involved in playing the one-armed bandits.

(2) *Staged "adultery."* Actually, this experience is from one perspective, the most non-immoral thing one could imagine. Nothing happens. Employed as part of a package fee the *dramatis personae* (the correspondent-elect, a photographer and an additional witness) arrive at a hotel, along with the putative defendant. The female lead dons a negligee; the door of the selected room, conveniently left unlocked, is opened; and the photographer takes his picture (perhaps he follows the usual pattern of his profession: "Just one more, please!"). The additional witness simply looks on. This neat "evidence" is brought before the referee, who, in effect, decides such

matters; and it is said that there is a "canned" list supplied the plaintiff in such cases as to what questions are to be asked in precisely such a situation. The fact is, as F. Benjamin McKinnon has pointed out, the real case of adultery is much more difficult to establish than the play-acting.[9] It is suspected that the referees prefer the latter type because it contributes better to the court record of cases handled per month.

(3) *"Where are you?"* Then there is the Enoch Arden law. Here the plaintiff avers that the other spouse has not been heard of for five years. When involved in a divorce by mutual consent, this ignorance as to whereabouts can be affirmed with relative safety by the plaintiff-spouse; but an obvious difficulty with this particular device is that five years is sometimes a long time to clarify the status of a dead marriage.

(4) *The fake annulment.* As is found true in the ecclesiastical scene, when divorce is limited, annulment grows bigger. In New York State there are some one hundred and fifty types of fraud that have been claimed in annulment actions. A frequent and easy form of fraud (where there is mutual agreement to dissolve a marriage) is the pleading that there was no intent on the part of the husband and/or wife to have children (of course, this one doesn't stand up too well if, in fact, there are children).

At first blush, one is inclined flatly to condemn all this. But given the existential situation in New York, I am not so sure. Could there be in the development of one or more

[9] "Ethical Problems in Divorce Practice" (1957, unpublished essay).

of these "ways round" simply the carrying on of the legal
tradition of fictions? Suggestive here is the development
of the common law action of ejectment. In order to establish a suit for determining the title of property there
was at first a bit of playacting, the actors testifying in
the court their choreography; but it wasn't long before a
play was not in fact performed, but simply recited in the
plaintiff's pleading. By this time, it would have been
thought gauche were the defendant (as in the story in
which the child finally exclaims, "The King has no
clothes") to defend on the ground that the show really
never went on. It started like staged adultery: someone
was hired to trespass on the property, while someone else
was hired to chase him off, etc.; and long after the events
no longer were required to occur, the pleadings were required to affirm the "events." We can say that one or
two or three of the above devices are fictions in a stage
of development where obviously the development has
not gone as far, for example, as in ejectment. Now something—not the real thing—simply has to happen "with
pix"; people still have to be hired. But it is beyond the
realm of legitimate projecture to assume that in connection with this device there may occur the second and
third phases in the development of suits to try title. The
second stage: it really didn't have to happen, it only had
to be pleaded. The third stage: when the Code procedure
came in, the little tale didn't even have to appear in the
pleadings.

Meanwhile, a lawyer seeking to achieve a marital dissolution (and we are still assuming that in the given case
the idea is a sound one and he is in good conscience in
the matter) has to raise this question with himself. Is

this fiction or fraud and perjury? In his profession, he is accustomed to dealing with the former category, but he certainly doesn't want to get involved in the latter category. This is an example of Man in Transition. I must confess that personally—or perhaps because of my ecclesiastical role—I am somewhat put off by the staged adultery fiction/fraud; yet, existentially speaking, what is the difference (except for its "sexy" connotation) between this and a long expensive trip to Reno? No less than a United States Supreme Court justice has expressed this kind of realism in at least one instance. The Virgin Islands tried to bid for what McKinnon calls "the tourist-divorce trade" and at the same time avoid the necessity of perjury involved in the usual migratory divorce. The Virgin Islands' law allowed the judge to eliminate any question about intention to remain (having gotten the tourist business out of the visitor they decided to let him depart in peace). The majority of the court blocked this attempt, but Mr. Justice Clark—joined by Mr. Justice Black and Mr. Justice Reed in his dissenting opinion—said:

> Divorce is an intensely practical matter, and if a husband and wife domiciled in any State want a divorce enough, we all know that they can secure it in several of our States. This being true, I see no sense in striking down the Islands' law. There is no virtue in a state of the law the only practical effect of which would be to make New Yorkers fly 2,400 miles over land to Reno instead of 1,450 miles over water to the Virgin Islands.

> The only vice of the Virgin Islands' statute, in an

uncontested case like this, is that it makes unneces-
sary a choice between bigamy and perjury. I think
the Court should not discourage this [the attempt
to make such a choice unnecessary] and I would reverse.[10]

To return to such a fiction/fraud as staged adultery:
in terms of the social outcome, is it better to require the
long trip to Reno rather than simply to require them to
take the shorter trip to a second-rate Manhattan hotel?

Speaking of the existential conditioning of law by so-
ciology, it is interesting to note these phenomena:

1. New York is only one state out of fifty (though the
most populous—temporarily, since my own state of California is soon to assume that place) and one third of all
the annulments granted in the Nation emit from the New
York courts.

2. Nevada is about the most relaxed state as to grounds
of divorce, yet for the real residents of that state, there
is one of the lowest divorce rates in the Nation.

The purpose here is not to solve the problem of marriage and divorce in this country. Time has been spent
on this particular problem in order to illustrate the complexity of the decision-making of the lawyer in regard to
field after field, should he take a conscientious view of
what he will or will not involve himself in, and what
means he will use to achieve given objectives. Earlier it
was insisted there is a question; it is now evident that it
is a tough one.

[10] Page 28 of Granville-Smith *v.* Granville-Smith in *United
States Reports, Cases Adjudged in the Supreme Court at Octo-
ber Term, 1954,* Volume 349, pages 1–28 (Washington, D.C.:
United States Government Printing Office, 1955).

But by this time in the analysis, some are bound to rechallenge the fundamental presupposition. When we have reached this point in discussions on this subject in which I have participated, someone usually says: "All this confuses me. Wrestling with such ambiguous and paradoxical questions will interfere with business. And as to the cases I would take, it would keep me from wholeheartedly and effectively serving my clients. I would rather concentrate on serving the professed needs of my clients." Some put it more bluntly: "I may lose my clients if I am too stuffy about such matters."

The only answer to this is a question, What does the lawyer put first in life? Now no matter how nobly he would like to answer this, he has something to weigh out. He should know that there is nothing unworthy in keeping in the picture the question, What will this do to me? And this is particularly so where the lawyer is responsible for the support of others. The lawyer with even the most dedicated sense of his total calling cannot fail to take into account his chances of staying in the game in order to exercise that calling; all this must be taken into account. Also to be considered is the continuing relationship with a given client. Perhaps he genuinely feels the relationship of trust he has been building up, enabling him to influence the client for good in his various decisions, and hence he may well hesitate to bolt the client whom he feels in a given instance to be pursuing an unworthy end.

For an idealist in ethics (one who would be a pacifist in the problems of war and peace) there can be no room for considerations such as these. The one who recognizes that those choices beyond the obvious ones are not a choice between black and white but between shades of gray—and I believe that this approach is true to sound Judeo-Christian ethics[11]—know there *is* room for such considerations, and many others like them. The degree to which any one of them is legitimate is a factor that cannot be judged simply by stating the factor. Whether such a concern is craven or responsible depends upon an inward matter—"purity of heart." And motives are capable of being so mixed in complicated decision-making, especially when we have taken into account the role of the unconscious mind, that in the end we must confess that only God knows all that is involved in the makeup of our decisions. Certainly in this no man can judge for another, or in any final sense as to himself. It was in this connection that Saint Paul said, "But with me it is a very small thing that I should be judged by you or by any human court. I do not even judge myself."[12] But there is true integrity to the degree that a person will seek to assess these matters, as far as may be, with purity of heart. But the lawyer will be less than a whole person if he does not at least raise these questions. If he is not disturbed and tormented by such things, then he is less than a whole person. And when what he has decided to do is in fact a shade of gray, at least he should realize that that is what he has done and not be under the illusion that he has chosen white. He will be deepened as a person by the very struggle of conscience through which he has arrived at his answer.

An attorney's being that kind of professional person is

[11] This thesis is more fully developed in *Doing the Truth*.
[12] I Corinthians 4:3.

sheer gain—in his personal life and for society. And it is not at all clear that in the long run he will suffer in terms of professional success. These very concerns are all along making him into a better person; and as he reflects these concerns in his consultations he will be gaining the respect and trust of more people while he may be losing attractiveness to some. The very fact that he is evoking these deeper considerations in his clients will make him a more trusted counselor and more respected as a man. Hence such an approach is more likely to contribute to his success professionally than to inhibit it. But everything would be spoiled if that should become the motive for his being that way. If anyone should decide that this higher approach is the secret of success in legal practice, then it won't work as such. It is genuine purity of heart, the honest concern in the struggle that is most winsome—not a feigned one, not the one that is "in order to." Directly applicable are the words of Jesus: "Instead, seek His kingdom, and these things shall be yours as well."[13] He did not say, "Seek His kingdom in order that these things shall be yours."

If the attorney will recognize the complexity of the decision-making process, and recognize his responsibility to make decisions beyond the requirements of the minimum, and in choosing the shade of gray recognize that he has not chosen the perfect good—thus protecting him from fanaticism and self-righteousness—he may well find that he is all the more successful. And, if it comes about that way, that's good, too. God is happy when we prosper. He wants us to be fully ourselves, and to have things turn out well for us.

[13] Luke 12:31.

V

The Lawyer as Pastor

A wise physician said some years ago to a joint conference of medical and theological students, "If I as a whole person am not treating a patient as a whole person, I might as well be practicing veterinary medicine." This applies to the lawyer's profession, too. Referring first to the subject of the physician's sentence, you should not separate yourself as lawyer from what you are as you. You should not seek to bifurcate your life into the eight-plus hours a day engaged in legal practice and what you are as a person the rest of the time. And to turn to the object of the physician's sentence, when a client comes in as a prospective plaintiff or defendant in litigation, or comes seeking to organize a scheme or to write a will, what has come in is not just a legal problem but a person with a legal problem, or a person who thinks he has a legal problem, or a person who is verbalizing in terms of a legal problem but may be in deeper need.

Analogous is what sometimes happens to pastors. A

person comes in and raises a narrow little question, for
example, "Why don't we sing more familiar hymns?" or
a somewhat abstract one, "I don't quite understand the
doctrine of the Holy Ghost." If one refrains from giving
a snappy, neat answer and listens long enough he may
find that a whole life is falling apart. The specific question may be put in your hand on the end of a string that
can lead you in from the anteroom of professed concern
into the larger room of real concern. If such a person is
allowed to articulate, he may well come out with what
is really bothering him.

And so it can be with the lawyer. Some may retort,
"All that is none of my business. I'm not a priest; I'm a
lawyer and I prefer to keep things on that professional
level. Let the client state what he's come for and I will
try to deal with that forthwith." Such an attitude will
narrow the life of a lawyer, will make it very confining
—and in the end rather dull and mechanical. Think how
much a lawyer with such an attitude misses in his daily
work. Each client is an individual, peculiar (in the best
sense of the word) person, and how uniquely fascinating
every person is when really known.

True, not all that is perceived can be good or enjoy-
able. And this is true in any form of counseling—pastoral,
legal or psychiatric. A member of the latter profession
was counseling a difficult woman, and with great patience, but finally he lost his patience and said to her,
"Madam, you don't have an inferiority complex: you're
inferior." But if the counselor can stick with it—if he can
take it—in the end he will find there more of interest, of
value, and even of splendor, than he suspected.

Legal counseling is simply a form of human interrelationship. In such, communication is never at its best when it is station-to-station. It is better person-to-person. Hence, simply because he is called to be a whole person, every lawyer is called to be a pastor. He is called upon to listen; he is called upon to help clients see the truth, to raise the right question in connection with the whole view of the matter involved.

But this is not a calling to run other people's lives. There is one thing that bothers lawyers when this pastoral claim is laid upon them. They will say in effect, "Who am I to play God for the client?" The answer is, "You certainly should not—nor should any priest, minister or rabbi, for that matter." A good pastor (in the narrower sense of the word) does not tell his counselee what to do; he tries from his overall perspective, and his knowledge of the person, and his grasp of the situation to see what the fundamental nature of his professed problem is, to help the counselee take all factors into account and evaluate them soundly. On the one hand, he seeks to lift burdens that the person may have unnecessarily imposed upon himself, and, on the other, to stimulate the person to a recognition of real obligation. He seeks to help the person see through his own rationalizations, defense mechanisms, etc. He may suggest possible harm to the counselee or others from a proposed course of action or from a deflection from a course of action. If such a legal counselor senses needs beyond his own depth he will seek to make sound referrals, carrying through, where it is appropriate, as a helpful collaborator with that other professional.

Quite analogous is the role of the lawyer as pastor. He certainly is not expected to tell the client what to do, but he is morally bound to give the best of himself to the client as a person, not simply as the carrier of some legal business.

Whitney North Seymour, formerly President of the American Bar Association, in indicating that a "reappraisal of the lawyer's role in advising his clients is desirable," develops the point this way:

> . . . As a result of the growth of business and of government regulation, have we become so accustomed to simply telling our clients what the SEC or the antitrust regulations are that we fail to tell them what they ought to do in the light of their moral responsibilities to the community, to their competitors, to their employees, and to themselves? Whatever may have been the case at the peak of the industrial revolution, I am inclined to think that lawyers have begun to swing in the direction of taking a larger view of their obligation in advice to clients.
>
> I think that the business corporations of this country, perhaps as a result of the series of blows that have been rained upon them in the last twenty-odd years, and the advice of public relations people and the growth of a new generation of executives, have begun to feel themselves that they ought to look at the whole panorama in charting their courses. Many of them recognize a public responsibility going beyond bare legal rights. As a result their lawyers have been encouraged to give a broad kind of advice. That is a good thing. It does seem to me that the

city lawyer at his desk, just as a country lawyer, visualizes his client's problem not only as a question of when the Statute of Limitations runs, but, in looking to his community, how his moral responsibility will be carried out, and how many nights he is going to spend feeling remorseful if he makes a judgment which is really not fair.[1]

In short, as he points out, "We all know that our maximum contribution is made when we can give the broadest kind of advice. That is true of business corporations, but it is more true of individuals."

In addressing myself to this subject here I am in a sense carrying coals to Newcastle. One of the faculty, Professor Howard R. Sacks, was kind enough to share with me an outline, "Talking with Clients," prepared for the seminar in interviewing and client counseling. Based on sound presuppositions and a noble concept, it sets forth with specificity and realism various aspects of the counseling process, with insight from other disciplines and sensitivity to human considerations. I hope that this thirty-six-page outline will be widely read and that seminars of this type will be participated in by more and more students in more and more law schools and eventually will become part of the increasingly popular in-service training in advanced law school instruction for lawyers already in practice.

Since I am, in effect, filing this document "by title" as part of this book, I will simply seek to summarize certain

---

[1] "Religion and the Law" in *Man at Work in God's World*, pages 152–153.

aspects of the pastoral relationship of attorney to client.[2]

Much of this process—and the limitations upon it—are not only common to several professions, as I have indicated; they are common to the relationship of friend to friend. Any good counselor will try to help the counselee understand the issues at stake, try to free him from compulsions, fanaticism and irrationality, in the hope the person himself will make a sound decision.

The field in which this can all be seen most easily is that of domestic relations. As Mr. Seymour has said, "when we are consulted by individuals about their family problems, the broader advice we can give, the more complete the pastoral relationship, the better the lawyer's work is."[3] For example, sometimes a client who comes in with a direct question, "How easily can I get a divorce, and how quickly?" really doesn't want a divorce but he wants to gain possession of a big stick he can take home. He is hoping to be able to say, "Now, look, change your behavior or I'll get a divorce—and I've just found out how." Now, as to whether that is the best thing for the client to do when he gets home is a question the lawyer cannot really ignore if he has any way of discerning what the client really has in mind. And sometimes the client is moved into taking the initiative because he fears that his spouse will, even though he is little inclined to want a breakup of the marriage. Sometimes two lawyers have been brought into the act and things string along

[2] Because of the genuine pastoral character of this role of the lawyer we arranged to have Professor Sacks lead two sessions in this field at our last Diocesan clergy conferences.

[3] *Op. cit.*, page 153.

to a finale that neither party really wanted—where there is real substance to the marriage, but where frustration and pride and fear have come to dominate the scene.

Sometimes the two lawyers can work together to save the reality. We all know that it is a violation of the canons of legal ethics for two lawyers in a given matter to connive disloyally against their clients. But while for lawyers to connive in this kind of situation may seem to represent disloyalty to the verbalized aims of the clients, it actually may be true loyalty to their real aims. In this connection a very touching incident once occurred. I knew a couple once whose marriage had gotten snarled up. Their pastor had given up on reconciliation, but a pair of sensitive lawyers made the grade. Each had tried, with non-directive counseling with the spouse who was his particular responsibility, but each party had his chin up and it appeared that the divorce would have to be carried through. When virtually all had been arranged and agreed upon, the lawyers cooked up a little scheme. Each told his client that since everything else was now settled, it would simplify the concluding of the process if for the determination of the distribution of furniture, wedding presents, and items they had purchased together, etc., they meet in a private room in one of the lawyers' offices and work out a check list to their mutual satisfaction. It is not hard to guess what happened. As they began to talk about a silver tray given them by life-long friends, a much-enjoyed antique they had found together in a little shop, a rug they had bought "on time," they realized through these material symbols how many abiding ties as to persons and to things they really had. It was not long before both were in tears and decided to call the whole thing off. When the husband timidly went out to seek the counsel whose space they were using in order to pass the word, he found both lawyers there and ready for congratulations to the couple—and for the subsequent celebration. These two lawyers received a much lower fee, because there was no litigation; but their reward was beyond price. Whatever may have been the religious orientation of these two counselors-at-law, in this holy scheme they exemplified Jesus' injunction to be "wise as serpents and innocent as doves."[4]

Again, the same old question comes up. Will this kind of dealing with clients put them off? Any answer in a given situation would be colored very much by the degree of trust the lawyer has evoked in the client, the psychology and morality of the client himself, and the way the lawyer has handled himself. It is indeed possible for the lawyer to be too directive in his counseling. The negative feeling that some lawyers have toward pastoral approach is a good half-truth: no man should seek to dominate the life of another. Assuming that the lawyer is keenly aware of this limitation, by and large his larger scope of concern will not put off clients. Not only in the realm of domestic relations, but in every kind of problem that is brought into the office, the client is in real need as a person and is not far from knowing it. He verbalizes the matter to his attorney in terms of getting some money that is rightly his or avoiding paying some money he shouldn't pay or "I simply want my rights" or "I am not going to be taken advantage of," when actually there are deeper currents moving in his spirit. Feelings have

[4] Matthew 10:16.

been hurt, or there is a desire to get revenge, status symbols are involved, there is a desire to re-establish one's own self-esteem, or to make a point. And though he may have complained to many people about the matter, he may not yet have run into a truly objectively concerned person until he has reached your office. In your whole calling—not just your legal calling—you have been anointed to be that person, that concerned person. This is not merely obligation, it is an opportunity. Just think, you have the chance to be that person, to be a true pastor. Abstractly speaking, you ought to be this all over the place. Not many of us can; each of us is finite. God is ready with grace for anyone who seeks it; but we cannot be so available. But here the man is, he is right there. There is your chance to be your full self, and to help him to be. Each such opportunity is a chance of a lifetime. Nothing like this will ever happen again. Take it, with all you have. This particular role as the role we discussed in the last chapter is part of the lawyer's calling. This is his vocation as a human being. And we can leave to God the increase, as those who will recognize His full claim on their lives are thus related to other lives, as opportunity affords.

There are dangers in the process, as there are in other callings, such as psychiatry and the ministry. There is the danger, for example, of transference. He or she[5] can transfer the whole focus of being to the counselor. As we know from other fields of counseling, this is not necessarily a bad thing; it simply presents an amber light to

[5] Perhaps more often she, since in spite of the emancipation of women most lawyers are male.

the counselor. His own stability as a person, his own sense of motivation, is at stake here. Caution, yes. But you can afford to be "a leg up" for a person for a short time, until he can restabilize and find a more solid and thus fine foundation for living; and this role can bring grace both to you and to your client. One can hope that the client can transfer to a deep dimension of religious and ethical understanding, and perhaps here you can non-directively help. In any case you can hope that you will become personally disinvolved. But that for the time being if the person is attached to you as a savior (in whatever terms he may conceive) is a fragile representation of your role as a co-redeemer with God of mankind with its many hurts, frustrations, anxieties and sense of meaninglessness. As troublesome and sometimes dangerous as this can be, it is part of your work as one made in the image of God.

Before proceeding to consideration of the next role of the lawyer, it should be pointed out that there is a real unity in the two particular roles already considered: in the judgmental role in which one sits out and weighs out a matter presented to him before he proceeds to be part of it; his special relationship to clients in regard to the formation of their own purposes; in his balancing out of the value of the continuing relationship to a client as against his doubts as to whether he had better be involved in the given thing, weighing in consideration the future of his own career—not necessarily an evil concern; in his concern to be at least a good technician, and more than a technician, in his relationship to a person who comes in with a problem. In all this the lawyer is simply being himself as a person, as one who knows he is under a calling. As one can do this, weigh these things and be willing to engage in the struggle knowing that more often than not he will end up not with whites but grays, one is not necessarily compromising but fulfilling his personhood—indeed his imagehood of God—in a world that is a mixed bag. The man I fear is one who does not worry about any of these problems—either the one who sees things in black and white, due to his unmitigated self-righteousness, or the one who through diffidence doesn't care whether there is an answer or not. The man in the struggle, in the strain, in the humble and yet confident feeling after these things wishes to be all that he can be to those who he is serving—well, this is a lawyer already in the way of salvation.

VI

The Lawyer as Citizen

The concern of this chapter will be usefully focused through the medium of a letter written some years ago by a distinguished law school dean to the Ford Foundation. It is doubtless an overstatement, but in that very fact lies its shock value. It reads:

Generally speaking, I have found that the law student is not interested in enrolling for courses not considered valuable in terms of bar examinations or usefulness in actual practice. He is not interested in learning for its own sake. He feels that a course in legal ethics should be optional, not required, and has so little interest in such courses as legal history, jurisprudence, and comparative law as to make it seem undesirable at present to include them in the curriculum of a small school. He is not interested in literature, in politics (local or national), in world affairs, or in vital state legislative matters, at least to a degree which will induce him to attend lectures or discussions or debates on these subjects, even when law classes are excused to facilitate attendance. He has no particular interest in civil rights. He has only a limited and academic interest in the improvement of judicial procedure and would not, of his own volition, attend an evening meeting in the law school at which the best speakers in the state would gather to discuss this subject. He gives only passing attention to matters of such importance as the Bricker Amendment, the Formosan problem, or the situation of the United States respecting its "friends." And he does not become particularly interested or excited if the state legislature, or others, moves to restrict academic freedom in the state schools.

All this may seem a harsh indictment of the American law student, but experience indicates that it is true. The American law student is a fine person; but like our medical students, our engineers, and our business students, he is a specialist whose primary interest is in things material rather than in service and in acquiring wisdom and understanding. The law student is interested in acquiring a knowledge of law which will enable him to pass bar examinations, to obtain a good job, and to handle his clients' affairs with high proficiency. He has no corresponding interest in civic affairs, or in the welfare of society, except to the extent that it may concern him personally. . . .[1]

[1] Edward C. King, Letter (used with permission) to the Ford Foundation, March 1955. Dr. King is Dean of the University of Colorado Law School. Courses of the type indicated above as lacking are now offered there.

In light of the fact that so many law students are present at these lectures, especially this lecture on the very subject of social responsibility, perhaps we need not take quite so dim a view of the matter as the good dean does in his letter. Nevertheless, there is obviously a great deal of truth in it as is reflected in the diminution of the role of the practicing lawyer himself in public affairs, discussed in the first chapter. As has been pointed out, there have been periods where lawyers were among the leaders in the Nation, in their states and in their local communities, conspicuous in constructive broad-gauge thought and action in public affairs. In contrast I cited the attitude of some modern law firms that discourage or prohibit their members from this very participation. Even without such an explicit ban many lawyers indeed are in default in this regard, and they are well described by the words in the dean's letter. This is true of some attorneys because they seem to regard such involvement as indiscreet; it is doubtless true of others due to diffidence and apparent preoccupation with the professional work at hand. In either case it would seem not to be fully appreciated that there is a realm of moral responsibility in this regard.

My basic presupposition in this regard can be stated in the form of a syllogism:

> With greater capacity goes greater responsibility.
> Generally speaking, the attorney has greater capacity for sound leadership in public affairs.
> *Ergo*, he should get with it.

The major premise is so obvious a moral principle that it does not require elaboration. The minor premise is supported by the following considerations:

1. The very study of the law develops ability in logical analysis. Contrary to certain modern educational philosophies, I still hold to the school of pedagogy that affirms that a thorough study of certain types of specific fields can develop in the student general capacities for logical analysis. For example, I believe the study of mathematics or Latin syntax can develop the mind in its ability to analyze matters beyond mathematics and classical literature. The study of law is certainly such a subject. Alexis de Tocqueville, one of the penetrating French observers of American life in 1831 pointed out that "the lawyer serves the Nation because of his experience in the regular connection of ideas."

2. The lawyer, and I think this is even more true than of the student of political science, should have gained a profound grasp of the structures and the raison d'être of characteristic fundamental American institutions.

3. The lawyer is trained in distinguishing fancy from fact and in drawing conclusions from genuine evidence.

4. He is trained in the arts of persuasion, as contrasted with force, in the attaining of chosen objectives.

Actually those four things are the attributes most needed in any person exercising a responsible part in the development of public opinion in achieving a sound reform of society. The members of our profession have by the very nature of their study and legal practice, been especially blessed in these regards. Hence the special obligation that is laid upon us. To put it negatively, and somewhat homiletically, if we lawyers do not assume responsibility in this realm, who else can we expect to do it better? Comparison between given individuals is not intended; obviously non-lawyer X may in fact be more effective in public matters than lawyer Y. But speaking in terms of likelihood, I am sure that the conclusion is indisputable. There is no question but that the lawyer is specially vocated for this end. This special vocation extends beyond responsibility for concern for the reform of the law itself and the administration of justice—though a vocation in this regard is certainly primary, and obvious, in spite of the fact that many attorneys do not even concern themselves with this degree of social responsibility. Responsibility extends (with certain limitations to be pointed out later) the whole of all it touches in our corporate life in nation, state and community.

Not only has the lawyer a special role here, as has been established above; so does the law itself. While it is true that theology, ethics and mores have had a continuing effect in the shaping of the law and that the individual lawyer's religio-ethical perspective has a bearing on his day-to-day functioning as judge, pastor and citizen, the reverse is also true: the law itself as it has developed has had a marked influence upon religious thinking, ethical standards and the shaping of community life. This book is concerned principally with the bearing that religion and ethics should have in the law and the work of the lawyer. But we should not ignore the other side of the coin, and to this end I file by title the excellent work by Professor Edmond Cahn, *The Moral Decision*.[2]

---

[2] Bloomington: Indiana University Press, 1955. Mr. Cahn is Professor of Law at New York University.

Incidentally, this approach provides the answer to those who in their resistance to social change say, "You can't legislate morals!" This statement is only a half-truth. It is true, of course, that the passing of a law does not necessarily make a direct change in the hearts and minds of persons who have consciously or unconsciously held attitudes contrary to the spirit and objectives of the new legislation. But in another sense, you can legislate morals. Assume that in a highly segregated community (and as you know there are many in the North as well as in the South) a Fair Housing Law is passed. Before its enactment, those active against segregation are the queer ones, on the defensive against the accepted mores (and, in the minds of many people, the morals) of the community. After the law is passed, these latter now represent the norm and those in opposition are thrown on the defensive. To use the distinction portrayed in the Westerns, between the bad guys and the good guys, the categories are now reversed. Obviously this gives courage to the reformers, having changed their status in the fight. But even as to the status-quoers, the very existence of the law and its enforcement is likely to have a gradual formative effect on not only their conduct, but eventually even upon their inward attitudes and motivations. The law can provide a kind of incubator for the development of sounder and more wholesome notions not only in life and personal interrelationships as well as toward the specific subject matter covered by the given law.

Cahn does not oversimplify this point. He is aware that the law's effect upon the development of social policy and the ideas that make certain constructive social attitudes possible is both constructive and destructive. In this connection he provides a useful outline:[3]

Where the notion of good seems excessively:	*The good-in-law can supply:*	*But in law there is risk of:*
Abstract	Projection by virtue of drama	Contest of wits between trial lawyers
Vague	Precision	Absorption with technicalities
Neutral or Irresolute	Intervention and Decisiveness	Meddlesomeness, Attribution of Artificial Guilts
Utopian	Responsibility	Philistinism[4]

That the law itself be an effective force in providing these constructive forces for the shaping up of sound ideas into practicable adaptability without draining the ideas of their power and their dynamic is part of the role of the lawyer. We are called to help bring about what is so well defined in the second column above and in the process to help avoid the side effects listed in the third column.

The word "responsibility"—another way of designating the total claim that I sought to establish in the first chapter—is a word that happily is receiving a larger place in professional groups. In fact it is more and more form-

---

[3] *Op. cit.*, page 57.
[4] That is, diffidence toward change; standpattism.

ing the subject of conferences of professionals. Speaking
of "professional responsibility," Professor Robert E. Mathews of the Law School of Ohio State University says:

> A body politic made up of those with capacity to
> exercise a free and informed choice is an essential to
> any leadership entitled to be called "responsible."
> Beyond this, there must be persons capable of inspir-
> ing confidence, of formulating programs responsive
> to the needs of others, and of attracting voluntary
> adherence—persons of vision, imagination, and a
> deep sense of dedication to human welfare, persons
> with a capacity for adjustment as well as for decisive-
> ness in action. When these qualities are in happy
> combination, and only then, can we have a leader-
> ship that is responsible in the great American tradi-
> tion. There are those who identify leadership with
> position. Yet we have seen in high positions far too
> many incumbents who lack the first qualities of lead-
> ership. Positions bring responsibilities, afford oppor-
> tunities for leadership, but occupancy of a position
> is no assurance that the incumbent will be a leader.
> The practice of law is itself a position. . . .[5]

And then he stresses this important point:

> "Responsibility" is a word of ethical connotation.
> All leaders must be responsible for making choices
> between values; and the higher the position of leader-
> ship, the broader are the policy factors that are in-

[5] Robert E. Mathews, "Legal Ethics and Responsible Leadership," in *Conference on the Profession of Law and Legal Education, December 4, 1952* (The University of Chicago Law School),
page 32.

volved, the more frequent are what Lasswell calls the "severely sanctioned decisions." A choice between good and bad, better and worse, good and less good, is essentially an ethical choice. No leadership is free of ethical choices of this sort. No, nor is any lawyer either. . . .[6]

This kind of leadership has a specially important role in our American society where so much of what is achieved rests upon voluntary association. The support of this aspect in our society is not only due to the kind of Constitution and Bill of Rights we have; it has long been a sociological phenomenon in this country. De Tocqueville in his observations also pointed out here that it was between the authority of the state and the somewhat unorganized—and unreliable—kind of good that individuals might do, a layer of what we can call "voluntary associationism" through which much of what needs to be done gets done, happily reducing the degree to which governmental authority must act, on the one hand, and yet on the other hand, not leaving things simply with the anarchy of individual action or inaction. But this process does not just work automatically: its effective working depends upon there being enough people around who conceive their role as citizens in this way and who are qualified so to function. Henry L. Stimson, who was a lawyer, twice Secretary of War and once Secretary of State, has said:

Through many channels I came to learn and understand the noble history of the profession of the

[6] *Ibid.*, page 33.

law. I came to realize that without a bar trained in the traditions of courage and loyalty our constitutional theories of individual liberty would cease to be a living reality. I learned of the experience of those many countries possessing constitutions and bills of rights similar to our own, whose citizens had nevertheless lost their liberties because they did not possess a bar with sufficient courage and independence to establish those rights by a brave assertion of the writs of habeas corpus and certiorari. So I came to feel that the American lawyer should regard himself as a potential officer of his government and a defender of its laws and constitution.[7]

This particular role of the lawyer is not included in the usual oath taken for admission to the Bar, but interestingly enough, it is covered rather well in the initiation ceremonies of one of the legal fraternities: "Consider the importance of our profession. It calls upon you to be the preservers of freedom, the defenders of weakness, the unravellers of cunning, the investigators of artifice, the humblers of pride, and the scourgers of oppression."[8]

We now turn to a particular application of this responsibility—one that is not the only thing, but is perennially important, and particularly important now in light of the totalitarian-minded threats to it, and not only from the left—namely, freedom. "The American Proposition," said Archibald MacLeish, "is the proposition that

[7] Henry L. Stimson and McGeorge Bundy, *On Active Service in Peace and War* (Harper & Brothers, 1948), pages xxi–xxii.
[8] Initiation Ritual, $\phi\Delta\phi$ Legal Fraternity (1949), page 7 [published with permission].

if men are free to think for themselves and to believe as they think and to say as they believe—if men, all men, are free to make their own way by their own means to the truth which is true for them, each one of them—the world in which they live and which together they compose will be a better world: juster, stronger, wiser, more various. It is the most courageous, the most high-hearted of all propositions: the most daring, the most revolutionary of earthly acts of faith. It is, indeed, the one new and wholly revolutionary idea the world we call the modern world has produced, for it affirms the maturity of man as mind and spirit and rests its hopes for the future upon man's will."[9] And, Mathews reminds us that "we of the learned professions are the natural and proper custodians of this proposition."[10] Again, this is the assertion of the simple proposition: the more capacity, the more responsibility.

Yet each one of us differs in speciality of capacity and the opportunities available to contribute toward development of democracy. Therefore, no man can judge another as to his activity or non-activity in this regard. One man's silence may be cowardice; another's, discretion—biding his time until he can get into a position where he can really count in the furtherance of the given concern. The same action in the case of one man may be due to courage, in the case of another it may be due to a choleric disposition. But we can't judge any man's motivations, nor can we expect the same thing from every man. But

[9] *Freedom Is the Right to Choose* (Boston: The Beacon Press, 1951), pages viii–ix.
[10] *Loc. cit.*

from every member of the Bar we should certainly expect some selected participation in public life, some real part in the corporate decision-making process. We should expect this of every citizen, of course; but especially we should expect it of these citizens, because of their specially sharpened tools.

We are in particular need of those who will be effective expositors and defenders of freedom. We are threatened by a whole ideology, one that is very effective in the world in terms of material resources and know-how in military prowess and which would, by intention, destroy all that which is basic to our system—and which we tend to take simply for granted. This is not simply another lecture in an anti-communism crusade, yet those of us who are nervous about the excesses of the professional anti-communists should nevertheless recognize that there is something there to be "anti-" and state our case for freedom on better presuppositions than those used by those who have made anti-communism their special calling. It is important that we not be merely *against* something, that we be *for* freedom. It is important that we understand the world view that makes it desirable and viable, and we must be convinced as to the soundness of the presuppositions that support it.

The premises for freedom are essentially theological and are grounded in the Biblical view of man, his nature, and his destiny. It is true that some of those who formed our institutions were currently influenced with French rationalism and philosophical deism—fads of the time; but this is of relatively little significance compared to the fact that the whole culture was drenched in the Biblical tradition. There are at least fundamental notions of the latter heritage in the fundamental development of our free way of life:

1. *A common Source of conscience.* Our forefathers were convinced that there is a policeman in every heart, and hence there needn't be a policeman on every block. This is the conviction that every man has a conscience and the Source of each man's conscience is the same; hence we can count upon a reasonably reliable pattern of social behavior without the imposition of a heavy-handed police state. All through history there are only two ways people have been able to have an orderly life together: they are either whipped together from the out-side or held together from the inside. We have counted upon these inner controls. Now without the belief on which this trust is based, the atheistic Communist system, quite naturally, is left with reliance on the former method.

2. *Original Sin.* I am not among those who believe that Original Sin is because of Adam and Eve; rather, Adam and Eve is because of Original Sin, that is, this myth developed rather late in the history of Hebrew literature (though it has ended up at the beginning of the Bible in the final editing of Genesis[11] and expresses in quite a sophisticated way the paradox of man's nature. Thus when asked, "Do you believe in Adam and Eve?" I answer, "Yes. I am Adam," for "Adam" is Hebrew for "a man"; the narrative is an Everyman play. On the positive side, man is all that the humanists claim for him—and more: he is basically creative (for example, he was given the right to name the animals and to have dominion over

[11] Genesis 2:15–3:24.

them: this is the relationship between science and technology: when man discovers what something *is* he can in the end run it. He is capable of a beautifully ordered and happy life (the Garden symbolizes this); he is capable of direct relationship with God (he walked and talked with Him) and his neighbor (typified by Eve), and he is at ease in this world and with himself (typified by his un-self-conscious nudity).

But there is another side to him equally basic. The serpent said to Eve, "You will be like God";[12] so men say, "I can run my own show"; "Watch out for number one"; "Ask no quarter and give none"; "Don't stick your neck out." This self-regarding, self-centering proclivity has expressed itself in the public field in terms of the danger of misuse of power. As the distinguished Roman Catholic historian, Lord Acton, said in a letter to Mandell Creighton, "Power tends to corrupt and absolute power corrupts absolutely."[13] The idea of our forefathers was not that man is so *good* that we should govern ourselves, but that man *can be so bad* that we dare not have a tyrant. Hence our doctrine of separation of powers, our system of checks and balances.

Institutions such as this are threatened when people forget the fundamental theological reasons for them. During the New Deal, the late President Roosevelt had control of the Executive Branch of the Government—and quite rightly so; he happened to have control of Congress; but the judicial arm was proving difficult: the Supreme

[12] Genesis 3:5.
[13] *Essays on Freedom and Power* (Boston: The Beacon Press, 1948), page 364.

Court was knocking out some of the emergency measures
he had put through. So he thought it would be well to
gain control of the Supreme Court as well and proposed
to add to its size sufficiently so that he could pack it with
enough men he could count on. It is fortunate that this
plan failed. A similar threat to fundamental notions is
also involved when legislative committees—such as the
House Un-American Activities Committee and the Senate
Subcommittee on Internal Security—which have a legitimate role in gathering data looking toward legislation, go
beyond that role and seek to "expose" (so the public see
it) individuals, leading to the loss of their jobs and
reputations.[14] Here they have entered the judicial realm,
but without judicial guarantees—for example, the right to
confront one's accusers, the right to cross-examine them,
the right to introduce independent testimony on one's
own behalf, checks on hearsay evidence, etc.

Now the Marxist theology has no doctrine of original
sin. Like the somewhat dated view of our American humanists (and some of our philosophers of public education), the Communists assume that "knowledge is virtue":
the man with the right ideas in his head will do the right
thing. The man thoroughly indoctrinated with the Party's
dogmas will faithfully execute the same. You might think
that they would have learned better by now: as you
know, there have been a number of purges and many a
Communist Party member has been given a one-way

[14] Cf. Watkins v. United States in *United States Reports, Cases
Adjudged in the Supreme Court at October Term, 1956*, Volume
352, pages 822 and 1022; Volume 354, pages 178–233 (Washington, D.C.: United States Government Printing Office, 1957).

ticket to Siberia. And there is also the naïve notion that when all works out right, and all the eschatology has come true, everyone will be so well-off and so happy that there will be no need of government at all. In this connection they should make a study of American suburbia, where there are a good many people quite well off who are not happy and even some of whom commit antisocial acts, requiring the intervention of government and even of the police. Their simplemindedness in this regard follows from the lack of a doctrine of Original Sin in their theological system.

3. *Eternal life.* Our forefathers believed that every individual was destined for eternal life, and that nations come and go. You read nothing in the *Federalist Papers* about "America forever." The Daughters of the American Revolution have sought to amend the fourth stanza of "The Star-Spangled Banner" to say "Then conquer we must, since our cause it is just, . . ." (now it says "when . . ."), but this is a recent aberration. Anyone who has read the Old Testament and seen the procession of Assyrians, Babylonians, Chaldeans, Persians, Antiochians, etc., or the New Testament, some of which was written after Israel's doom (for the time being), or subsequent history, where he has seen the fall of the Roman Empire and the Holy Roman Empire, etc., etc.—will realize that the time could come when the whole story of the United States of America is written up in a paragraph and a half in some grade school history book. The individual is more important than the State. He can last longer, indeed for eternity. Therefore his development, his ability to *be* himself, to articulate, to gather others around him and to seek to press his ideas is of the utmost

importance. This is all very precious in our American tradition.

Further, in this is the most important factor: the right of each individual to have an overview beyond the State, a stance from which to criticize the State, even when it would appear to be at its best. Therefore, it is in our best tradition when we put up with sore thumbs, rocks in the shoe, bulls in the china shop. We put up with inconvenient people. We recognize the right to be wrong—or what the majority may think is wrong.

But turn to the main other system. There the Communist State is eternal; and the individual dies like a dog. The priorities are completely reversed. Therefore the conclusion they have adopted is quite logical: tell the individual to "shape up or ship out"; brainwash him, orient him, use him. First things first.

This is a brief and oversimplified summary of the profound bases of a way of life that is unique on the face of the earth and that is being widely copied (all from the fundamental premises) by new striving nations. It is hard to be grasped even by the citizens of our own country, even by those who profess religiously—sort of *en bulk* —the general ideas that underlie it. We develop it in this chapter because those who can best grasp these connections and achieve a kind of consistency about them is the thoughtful attorney—particularly if he has read a little theology. Also, the lawyer should be the one most linked to the relationship of small trends to ultimate principles.

An editorial in the London *Times* of August 11, 1846, said this: "The greatest tyranny has the smallest beginnings. From precedents overlooked, from remonstrances despised, from grievances treated with ridicule, from powerless men oppressed with impunity, and over-bearing men tolerated with complaisance, springs the tyrannical usage which generations of wise and good men may hereafter preserve and lament and resist in vain. . . . Hence the necessity of denouncing with unwearied and even troublesome perseverance a single act of oppression. Let it alone, and it stands on record. The country has allowed it, and when it is at last provoked to a late indignation it finds itself gagged with the record of its own compulsion."[15] Watchfulness as to the eroding away of this concern for freedom is the special task of lawyers, and, where they are available, lawyer-theologians.

Actually this is not a one-way gift. True, we thus contribute something to society. But actually, it is through this kind of assumption of responsibility that we, with this special training and experience, are being formed and made as whole persons—which we are called to be. We should be familiar with the words of Sol Morton Isaac, once President of the Columbus Bar and President of the National Family Service Association:

How much of your time you should devote to the community and what this will do both for and to you and the community are unanswerable questions. But it is safe to say that whatever you do, as a lawyer or as a private citizen, will have more of an impact than you would now be inclined to believe—an impact both on you and on society.[16]

[15] Cited by Seymour in "Religion and the Law," *op. cit.*, page 143.
[16] "The Lawyer and the Community," Discussion of Topics relating to the Standards of the Legal Profession, Ohio State University College of Law, December 1, 1953.

These fine words elicit a question, particularly for those who are young lawyers or are anticipating being such: What effect will my word have? What difference will it really make what I say at a social gathering about a public question? How will even my most considered view count? As a lawyer for twenty-five years, let me reassure you that a single individual can have an amazingly large effect upon public opinion. But I have a particular complaint against the cocktail party. It provides the atmosphere, the company, and the stimulus (not to be overdone, please) for the discussion of public questions. Without this device, the Missouri Compromise was discussed in every hamlet in the Nation, yet today practically no one discusses the problem of Vietnam, where we are engaged in an undeclared war (and as a matter of fact the average attendant at a suburban cocktail party doesn't know where Vietnam is—whether it is near Israel or Korea). The opportunity is greater, but the function is less. What happens? "Where'd you go last summer?" "To our little spot near Provincetown. Where'd *you* go?" "Well, we have a nice quiet place on Lake Michigan." Actually, neither spokesman gives a hoot. This can be simply small talk to cover clumsy silences. Actually, small talk is good for slipping into important conversation and hence should not be minimized. But often it does not go beyond this, and simply strings out things at the same level. There is nothing positively wrong with any amount of this. What is wrong is negative: the loss of the opportunity for people to share their reflections on what's going on, the opportunity to develop in a small scale the basis of public opinion. When anyone breaks through on such an occasion, it is not distasteful: people *want* to talk about serious things.

Now who can better contribute on such occasions than
the lawyer? Let's take advantage of the illusions about
us: most people think that when we say something it
must be important. We know—or should know—that this
is not necessarily so, but let's use this prestige, at least
in so far as it help people *listen*. With the gifts of analysis
in which we have been especially trained, let's use the
opportunity. Other professionals have things to offer, but
they may be less useful than lawyers in this regard. On
social occasions, whatever we have to give, let's give it.

We who are professionals are still suffering under the
American stigma represented by the word "egghead." Do
you remember that terrible week when Sputnik I was
fired? That same week we had the official report of our
government on Russian education, which showed that
they were way ahead in the production of engineers and
in grammar school education of talented young people in
mathematics, science and languages. It was in that week
that a tremor of questioning our self-righteousness and
sense of superiority spread about the country. It was also
in that week that a brilliant cartoonist produced as his
caption, "What we need in this country are more egg-
heads and fewer fatheads."

Now I can finally use the word with which I wanted,
all along, to label this chapter, namely, "prophet." For
there is a call to be a prophet. Prophecy is not looking
into a crystal ball and emitting the details of future
events. True prophecy is looking at the here and now in
terms of an overarching perspective of things, including
the past and including, as far as one may perceive it, the
eternal meaning of reality. As a result, it is true that the
prophets often call the shots pretty well as to the future,

but that is secondary, and corollary, to their understanding of what is here and now.

The lawyer with his continuing involvement in a great tradition—of great antiquity and of great glory—should be able to see things in greater perspective than the fellow who simply reads the papers. Of course, there is no value in seeing things in perspective if one does not know what the facts are. There is a good Eleventh Commandment for both lawyers and clergy: "Thou shalt read carefully a good newspaper every day."

To effectuate some of these perceptions, the involvement in a political party is important. Yet, finally in his heart and mind, no one should be a "party man." Every man is called to be an "Independent" in the end. From his independent perspective, he may well decide to work through this or that party. He says, "I know what I am trying to push, and this would seem to be the best way to push it." But still in his soul and in his heart and in his mind he must be over and above it, with a critique of all things and all methods, with at the same time endorsive and affirmative attitudes toward all that is good and toward those who are seeking the good along with him.

This is the role of every person, really, but here again, I close where I started: With greater capacity goes greater responsibility. Hence we as lawyers are especially called to this role. We are especially called to the preservation of our way of life, to the endorsement of our freedoms, to the promotion of a sound public policy.[17]

[17] Cf. William S. Ellis, "The Christian Lawyer as a Public Servant," in *The Christian Scholar*, Volume 40, No. 3, September 1957, pages 194–210.

We of all people should be suspicious—and indeed negative—toward many attempts to solve things by label, by sneer. The leftists have been doing this for decades: Anyone a quarter of an inch to the right of the current line is a fascist, war-monger, colonialist, imperialist, etc. But similiarly, in the eyes of the radical right, if you are one quarter of an inch to the left of, say, the political position of President McKinley, you are a Communist, a Commie, a dupe of the Communists, a tool of the Communists. (The line keeps shifting. That's why there is a new definition of optimist and pessimist. You are an optimist if you are having your son learn Russian; you are a pessimist if you are having him learn Chinese. The Red Chinaman is the real fundamentalist; his is the "tent-meeting" form of Communism.)

The lawyer should be the last person to have any part of such labeling, from either direction. He should be piercing with his ability for careful analysis—a gift from God, which good law schools have helped him perfect.

VII

The Lawyer as Person

We have stressed the integral relationship between the attorney's professional life and his whole life as a person. We have considered the implications of a total claim upon him, in the various aspects of his work, in relationships with clients and to public concerns. Before we conclude, however, we should return to him *as a person* and consider what all this does to him. If my basic thesis is correct, we can safely state that it does three things. These are the same three things that, normatively speaking, would happen to anyone who takes seriously the main lineaments of the Judeo-Christian tradition, though of course the actual application is considerably shaped by the fact that a given man is a lawyer rather than a physician or an engineer.[1] And, further refining

[1] For other treatments of matters touched in this chapter see William Stringfellow, "The Christian Lawyer as a Churchman,"

this distinction, obviously the application will be somewhat different in the case of *each* lawyer, because of the utter uniqueness of each human being. But over and above particular applications, these same three things, in generic terms at least, do happen in the confrontation to which I have referred, and they are somewhat standard theological terms.

1. Judgment. No lawyer-reader will feel comfortable with the preceding pages, unless he is very adept at rationalization, because, stated poorly or well, the thesis is that there is an all-embracing claim on his whole being that far transcends the explicit structures of professional obligations. Before we consider the negative implications of such an assertion (such as an inferiority complex, or even despair) we should take note of the important positive thing: there is a joy and a glory in this. Judgment is part of the "good news" (which is rendered in Anglo-Saxon as "gospel"). Judgment means that the Ultimate Ground of the Universe (to use Paul Tillich's phrase) who has evolved all that has been evolved, who keeps the constellations in their courses, who keeps the law of gravity working, who sustains in existence all life and reality, *cares* what I do. This is the status symbol *par excellence.* This means that I matter; I am important. To affirm that what I do day by day matters to Him is to elevate every action or attitude into eternal significance. This gives to

---

in *The Christian Scholar,* Volume 40, No. 3, September 1957, pages 211–237; William S. Ellis, *loc. cit.;* and L. Harold DeWolf, "The Christian Vocation of the Lawyer," in *The Christian Century,* Volume 75, September 3, 1958, pages 993–994.

the various scattered moments of life—even to routine activities—a new charge, a new excitement.

On the other hand, a recognition of such a vast claim is bound to have a depressing effect, particularly if this were all that the Judeo-Christian tradition had to say. No one of us is all that good. No one of us—for a year, a month or even a day—has lived up to this claim. While the claim inspires us, it also condemns us. In the light of it, we see the shabbiness of some of our dealings, our schemes, our motivations. His bright light shows up a mixture of motives, unworthy compromises. He exposes our rationalizations. No wonder that, being human, we erect defenses. No wonder, being human, that we develop defense mechanisms, that through the Law itself we seek to modify, to reduce the claim to manageable proportions.

The fact is—and in itself it is a good fact—that virtually every lawyer wants to feel that he is not only a good lawyer (in the sense of technical proficiency) but that he is a lawyer of impeccable integrity. He not only wishes this to be his public image; he wishes to think this of himself. Self-acceptance is a very important element—perhaps the most important element—of a wholesome, serviceable personality. We naturally tend to seek self-acceptance by a shortcut, namely, by denial of the total claim or by rationalizations to support the conviction that we are conforming to the total claim. But this is not a sound —nor, in the long run, an effective—way to achieve self-acceptance. First, this approach dulls or even eliminates a healthy sense of self-criticism. Second, it does not get rid of a sense of inferiority and guilt; it simply suppresses

it in the unconscious mind and is unhealthy both spirit-
ually and physically (due to psychosomatic connections).[2]

2. *Grace*. If we really open ourselves to honest self-
criticism—often mediated through others—and drop the
false cover, another way of self-acceptance is available.

A fundamental motif of both the Old and New Testaments is that God is not only Claimant, He is also Redeemer. He manifests Himself not only in law but also in
grace. When we are willing to acknowledge what we are
really like, He will meet us where we are—take up the
slack between Himself and us. He will accept us—though
unacceptable, thus allowing us to accept ourselves. If
God accepts us, why should we not accept ourselves? For
Christians, this dimension of God's action is focused in
the Cross of Jesus Christ, but that God is this way and
that man has so experienced Him is portrayed throughout the Bible, from Genesis to Revelation, and permeates
the whole historic tradition of Judaism and of Christian-
ity.

It is the motif missing from the most exalted and ideal-
istic version of humanism. For those who can have confidence in the reality of Divine forgiveness and grace,
however, there can be a greater openness to exalted
claims and ideals. For, there will be less fear in finding
oneself humbled to the point of non-self-acceptance in
the attempt to fulfill them. But there is a further fruitage.

3. *Eucharist*. I am not here referring to the specific
liturgical service known as the Lord's Supper, the Holy

[2] See Chapters 2 and 3 in my *Beyond Anxiety*.

Communion or the Mass. I am referring to the motif behind these services and, as well, the literal meaning of the
word, namely, thanksgiving. The lawyer who accepts the
total claim and examines himself in the light of it, who
finds himself to have fallen short, only then goes further
and, through faith, accepts himself through the grace of
God—this lawyer now has a new motive for striving to
practice his profession and to fulfill all of his interpersonal
relationships—in the light of the total claim, namely, that
he is grateful for this free gift of acceptance. Now all the
more he will want to do what he is supposed to do.
Through this gift of grace, he himself will become more
gracious. He may indeed repeat the act. Having been met
where he is, he will be more inclined to meet others
where they are, not where he conceives they ought to be.
The slack having been taken up between God and himself, he will be more inclined to take up the slack between
himself and others. The hurt having been taken out of
his life, the more inclined he is to seek to take the hurt
out of the lives of others. Having been accepted though
unacceptable, he will be more accepting of others. Having been loved though not always lovable, he will show
more loving concern to others who may not be particularly lovable.[3]

This should do great things for him. But to return to
the caveat noted several times before in these pages,
doubtless this will make him more attractive and winsome as a person and will doubtless increase his clientele,
but all is spoiled should an attorney conceive of this as

[3] See Chapters 7 and 8 in *Doing the Truth*.

a means. Yet, it should not surprise him should greater success come as the fruitage.

Here more explicitly than anywhere else in these pages, we move beyond the ethical to the religious. We have not only touched on religion as that which ultimately lies behind ethics (whether explicitly or implicitly) but also as that which operates beyond the ethical by saying a word to one who, taking the ethics beyond legal ethics seriously, finds that he has fallen short and who through faith by grace (acceptance by God) has experienced a new dynamic for action, a new motivation for goodness, namely, thanksgiving. So this is not merely ethics nor ethics bolstered by religion. Pure religion, according to Søren Kierkegaard is this: the profound humiliation of man, the boundless love of God, and an endless striving born of gratitude. The canons of legal ethics will generally not produce the first step; however, recognition of the total claim should. Then the rest follows, through faith. If this is true religion, then lawyers should be among the most religious people. For the very grist of their mill presents more ambiguous situations calling for decisions than most persons are faced with. More than most people, they are bound to be involved in ethically mixed situations, where choices between shades of gray have to be made—with or without "purity of heart." Since they more than the representatives of most callings should feel the need of grace, they more than most should be able to experience the fresh motivation that comes from grateful response.

Yet, existentially speaking, this may not be the case. The degree that it is not so with lawyers is due to one of several reasons:

1. As to those professing to be believing Jews or Christians, there still may be discorrelation between what one expresses weekly in worship and how one functions throughout the week. Here we may parody the title of a popular film and sum it up as "Never on Monday." This may not be due in every case to the hypocrisy or moral weakness; it may simply reflect an innocence about the relationship of ultimate realities to daily living.

2. As to those who claim with pride or regret that they are not religious, there is a failure to recognize that every man *is* religious, that is, operates on a basis of premises taken on faith. However, with such, these premises may be examined and thus whether sound or unsound fail to operate with consistency.

3. A few—and I respect my brethren of the legal profession sufficiently to believe that there are very few—may have adopted consciously an egocentrism that says flatly, "I am for me." And from this flows expected actions and attitudes. But even here—because no man, whether because of social conditioning or grace of God, can be totally egocentric—their behavior is probably not as base as the basic premise would seem to imply.

In each case, however, we see a pointer to what is an important task for any lawyer. Let him give conscious and mature study to his world view, in the broadest sense, that is, his frame of reference, his perspective on life and reality. Whether he is a member of one of the standard-brand religions or not, let him take a new look at whatever it is he professes and at what set of premises he actually operates on. For instance, he may find that here he is a divided person, professing one system but actually living and working according to another. By using the adjective "mature" I am recognizing the fact that the lawyer is, generally speaking, a holder of a graduate degree; therefore, his exploration of religion should be on a graduate level. It is not enough either that he continue to prate what he learned as a child in Sunday School or that he assert a juvenile or undergraduate rebellion to what he learned in Sunday School. The most important thing about what he will be as a lawyer as well as a person will be his overarching world view. He certainly should take a fresh look at this no less seriously than he approaches particularized legal study and preparation. The level of his reading and thought and consultation on this subject should be "graduate."

There are several possible results from such a process. He may make more explicit what has been implicit; thus his general outlook will be more operative in terms of his particular decision-making, making him more consistent as a person. He may decide that the tradition in which he has been raised is the soundest one, but he will have deepened in it, and it will have more bearing on his daily life and his profession. Or, he may decide that what he has always unselectively accepted is an inadequate frame of reference for what he has experienced as a person— and as a particular kind of person, namely, one vocated to the law. Hence, he may consciously choose another religious posture.

Whichever of these results ensues, nothing but good can result. Finally, there will be conferred upon him an even greater sense of dignity to exercise our noble profession. He will see a greater meaning—and perhaps an eternal meaning—in that to which he is putting his mind and heart day by day. He doubtless will be blessed with

—and at the same time—more humility and more self-confidence. He will be more focused as a person—indeed, become a more effective and attractive person. If more and better business comes from this, fine. Regardless, his life will be more nearly fulfilled. Indeed, he may experience what in my newer profession we call salvation.

Index

E